The Changing Face of Catholicism

The Changing Face of Catholicism

Building a Church for the Future

Robert J. Hater

Paulist Press
New York / Mahwah, NJ

Scripture quotations are from New Revised Standard Version Bible: Catholic Edition, copyright © 1989, 1993 National Council of the Churches of Christ in the United States of America. Used by permission. All rights reserved worldwide.

Cover image by EvGavrilov / Shutterstock.com
Cover design by Sharyn Banks
Book design by Lynn Else

Copyright © 2024 by Robert J. Hater, PhD

All rights reserved. No part of this publication may be reproduced, stored in a retrieval system, or transmitted in any form or by any means, electronic, mechanical, photocopying, recording, scanning, or otherwise, without either the prior written permission of the Publisher, or authorization through payment of the appropriate per-copy fee to the Copyright Clearance Center, Inc., www.copyright.com. Requests to the Publisher for permission should be addressed to the Permissions Department, Paulist Press, permissions@paulistpress.com.

Library of Congress Cataloging-in-Publication Data
Names: Hater, Robert J., author.
Title: The changing face of Catholicism: building a church for the future / Robert J. Hater.
Description: New York; Mahwah, NJ: Paulist Press, [2024] | Includes bibliographical references. | Summary: "This book explores ways to develop vibrant communities of faith, centered in the parish and the home"—Provided by publisher.
Identifiers: LCCN 2023043039 (print) | LCCN 2023043040 (ebook) | ISBN 9780809156986 (paperback) | ISBN 9780809188451 (ebook)
Subjects: LCSH: Catholic Church—Social aspects. | Church renewal.
Classification: LCC BX945.3 .H38 2024 (print) | LCC BX945.3 (ebook) | DDC 253/.32—dc23/eng/20240213
LC record available at https://lccn.loc.gov/2023043039
LC ebook record available at https://lccn.loc.gov/2023043040

ISBN 978-0-8091-5698-6 (paperback)
ISBN 978-0-8091-8845-1 (e-book)

Published by Paulist Press
997 Macarthur Boulevard
Mahwah, New Jersey 07430
www.paulistpress.com

Printed and bound in the
United States of America

I dedicate this book to my family. Stanley and Olivia Hater, my parents, taught my sisters, Mary Ann Haubner and Joan Kohl, my brother, Thomas, and me the way of faith through their dedication, good example, and love. My siblings provided me with the support necessary to follow the path of the Lord in my ministry.

In addition, I dedicate it to Sr. Ann VonderMeulen OSF, Carol Smith, Sr. Frances Hogan OSU, Don and Cheryl Dresmann, Sigrun Haude, Marian McSwigan, Christina Hazlett, along with Rev. George P. Jacquemin and the entire staff at St. Clare Church, Cincinnati, Ohio.

CONTENTS

Foreword by Angela Ann Zukowski ix

Acknowledgments xiii

Introduction xv

Part I: Influences of Contemporary Culture 1

1. Challenges from the Digital World 5
2. Changing Perspectives in a Troubled World 17
3. New World Possibilities 26

Part II: Changes in the Church and Society 37

4. Family, the People of God, and Community 41
5. Active Leadership 53
6. Pope Francis and Pastoral Leadership 61
7. A Mission-Focused Church 67

Part III: The Future of Catholicism 77

8. Looking Ahead 79
9. A New Awakening of Faith 88

Contents

10. Vibrant Parishes, Faithful Families 100

Conclusion 108

Selected Bibliography 111

FOREWORD

Reading *The Changing Face of Catholicism*, I am reminded of the book *Communicating Christ to the World* (1994) by my friend, Cardinal Carlo Maria Martini. Cardinal Martini was a powerful communicator raising minds and hearts to the impact of the evolving communications milieu for communicating faith.

This book expands Martini's observations for a twenty-first century comprehensive perspective for understanding the impact of the digital milieu amid the challenges facing the Catholic Church today.

The author's many years of leadership and ministry are reflected throughout these pages. He manages to capture the breadth and depth of rapid digital cultural changes challenging every dimension of the Catholic Church's life and ministry. His writing is in sync with conversations emerging from the Synod on Synodality (2023–2024) and the theme of Pope Francis's 2024 World Day of Communications: "Artificial intelligence and Wisdom of the Heart: For a Fully Human Communication."

The author addresses relevant topics, issues, and trends synthesizing our lived experience within the Church. He weaves personal stories to demonstrate how evangelization needs to take shape and form within a shifting milieu. For example, he states, "Today, people desperately need to experience a sense of community that is often missing in their lives."

The Changing Face of Catholicism

My observation based on dialogue with university students or in giving parish presentations resonates with Hater's experience. People are in search of a deeper sense of community, as Hater notes, "that cares about them and can help provide their lives with spiritual meaning. A parish community that is hospitable, welcoming, and compassionate is more attractive than a parish that is administered efficiently."

This resonates perfectly with the Final Document of the Synod on Synodality (2023). Here, we read, "Synodality is a great source of hope for renewing and strengthening communion. The hope is that by becoming more synodal, the Church, as one delegate described, would be 'safe places where people can ask their real questions about Church teaching without judgment or punishment' (Session X Group 8)" (32).

The chapter addressing leadership styles also resonates with current pastoral conversations as dioceses explore the future of parish life via merging and amalgamation. The author highlights the two types of leaders: transformational and transactional. He encourages us to discern the styles of ecclesial/parish leadership required for moving forward as a vibrant, inclusive parish. As Pope Francis stresses the importance of dialogue, accompaniment, and engagement, Hater articulates practical questions inviting us to discern proactive, prophetic initiatives for implementing these ideas. This is the pathway forward for nurturing a new way of being Church.

Each chapter ends with thoughtful questions to invite us to explore deeply the ways we can make a difference in our evangelization initiatives in line with Pope Francis's pastoral vision for the Church.

We are reminded throughout the book that "we live in a new world, and the future Church demands new modes of

Foreword

presence and interpersonal communication." Chapter 10 offers practical guidelines for parish leaders and ministers to commence their journey for becoming a vibrant, inclusive parish faith community.

Angela Ann Zukowski, MHSH, D.Min.

ACKNOWLEDGMENTS

I acknowledge the insightful suggestions and critiques from Rev. John R. Civille, Sr. Ann VonderMeulen, OSF, Ms. Jeanne Hunt, and Mary Ann Haubner while I was writing this book. I am especially grateful for the wise suggestions and skilled editing of Paul McMahon of Paulist Press in bringing this book to completion.

INTRODUCTION

Change is inevitable and changes in the Church have happened from the beginning. Reflecting on change reminds me of an episode when my family went on a vacation to Holland, twenty-eight years ago. My grandmother came from there, and Mom often expressed a desire to visit the place of her birth.

While in the Netherlands, we attended Sunday Mass in a large, old parish church. We were surprised at the few people in attendance, interspersed throughout the church. Most attendees were over sixty years of age. This was in stark contrast to the many people of all ages attending Mass in the United States.

This Dutch parish came to mind recently. Who would have dreamed that, years ago in Holland, I experienced a foretaste of what is now happening in U.S. parishes with a significant drop in attendees at Sunday Mass. As I reflect on current Mass attendance, I think of the empty pews in our parishes and ask myself: What will the future hold?

This question gives us pause to wonder if future generations of Catholics will maintain active involvement in our changing Church. Without a doubt, the future Church in the United States will be different from the past. How different depends largely on us.

As you read this book, remember that contemporary culture contains many challenges and a hodgepodge of issues, beliefs, and practices. Key ones are addressed here, but to treat all of them would be impossible. Ambiguity prevalent in the broader culture is reflected in our analysis of how the Church deals with these issues.

Looking to the future, we stress basic actions that the Church must take instead of giving answers to new situations. Consequently, a future Church must be flexible, welcome everyone, and tolerate diverse opinions, while working toward unanimity of belief and practice.

The Changing Face of Catholicism considers changes currently taking place in the Church and the highly digital culture that challenges it. Appreciating the impact of culture is key to ascertaining the future vibrancy of Catholicism. To ensure the Church's health, our family, parish, and church leaders need to link Christ's message to deeper questions, such as: What is the meaning of life? Where do we find love? Do we offer a sense of welcome? How do we cope with sickness, suffering, and death?

For Catholicism to be vibrant in the future, it must couch Jesus's unchanging teachings within the changing contemporary digital, scientific, and technological culture. Our younger generation assimilates this culture, as children grow up with television, cultural shifts, and digital technology, while many older people struggle to identify with it.

When we consider the age-old truths taught by Jesus within the context of this new digital world, it becomes clear that changes in our Church and secular culture are needed. Furthermore, this process sheds fresh light on the relationship between church and culture and helps us see that every culture has its own way of viewing reality.

Introduction

To better appreciate the relationship between culture and the Church, we consider paradigm shifts—a major shift in a world view or perspective, which offers us a new way of seeing and doing things—that have occurred in both the Church and society throughout the past hundred years.

Paradigm shifts are often the result of new information that creates inconsistencies within the current paradigm. Pope John XXIII saw this happening in the Church and called for the Second Vatican Council (1962–1965), which introduced liturgical and other changes into the life of the Church. This event and the changes it brought influenced the Church's growth as it began to examine its role in the modern world from a fresh perspective.

Today, differences exist between Catholics who identify with the changes begun at Vatican II and those who question them. What emerges will depend largely on how the Church takes the best of Vatican II and balances it with the new insights that continue to emerge.

To succeed, the Church must adapt to new ways and communicate these changes effectively. The key is to maintain the essentials while incorporating fresh directions for the Church.

The decrees of Vatican II ushered in a new relationship with the modern world. This relationship requires continued dialogue with changing world perspectives, especially through the digital media that offers the Church new challenges and opportunities to share the message of Christ. The changing world perspective is not unlike the transition from an oral to a written culture that occurred in medieval times.

The first part of this book considers the digital influences of secular society on the Church. The second part considers

The Changing Face of Catholicism

how the Church might address these influences if it is to remain a vibrant, spiritual presence in society. The third and final part considers the future of Catholicism. Each part includes questions for individual reflection and group discussions and invites us to consider how today's influences will affect future generations.

Part I
Influences of Contemporary Culture

Secular society bombards us with materialistic ideas and various moral attitudes. I became acutely aware of its influence one day before giving the keynote address at a ministry conference. The realization happened as I was being driven from the airport to the cathedral, where I was to speak.

As we drove through the heart of the city, large skyscrapers lined both sides of the street, giving us the feeling that we were in a huge tunnel. The buildings, mostly glass in front, painted a beautiful picture of a contemporary secular city. As we passed by them and looked ahead toward the cathedral, I thought, "We are driving through the cathedral of today." These large, well-constructed, and easily accessible buildings housed banks and financial institutions.

The setting symbolized the modern city and its influence on contemporary society at its best. Within the walls of these buildings, the employees played their part, making sure that the business was successful.

When we neared the cathedral, the setting changed. We were now in the older section of town that had once been the center of business activity. It was here that farmers and cattleman used to bring their produce and wares to the market. The cathedral area was beautiful but markedly different from the glass-lined business district.

As we left the business district, we saw a symbol of today's digital secular culture. It was a massive painting of an iPhone on the wall of a six-story building, reminding us of our contemporary lifestyle.

The next morning, at the keynote address in the cathedral, I alluded to the lifestyle reflected in the glass-lined city outside, and asked, "How can the Church bring faith into the twenty-first century?" and "How does the Church remain new and fresh and make the cell phone, painted on the building, a symbol of blessing, not a barrier to realizing that life is more than money and finances?" This book hopes to shed light on both these questions.

This experience reinforced my awareness that to touch the depths of the human person in today's world, we must do what Christians have always done, namely, connect Jesus's message with people's real-life experiences. This applies particularly to our youth, who look for stability and a meaningful road map that makes sense.

When social media bombards us with secular dreams, it becomes difficult to sift out conflicting opinions that cloud the road ahead. It is in these moments that young people, especially, look for a welcoming spirit from the Church and a positive and enthusiastic response from its leaders. They need to

Influences of Contemporary Culture

hear about Jesus. As we realize that life is more than money, power, and sex, Jesus becomes alive in our lives and his message begins to bear fruit.

Society, strongly influenced by its digital media, affects all of us. It seeps into our bones and affects our attitudes and beliefs. Furthermore, if Catholicism hopes to play a significant role in shaping the attitudes and beliefs of future generations, it is imperative to face the growing challenge of atheism.

We begin by addressing the challenges of the secular world and ascertaining what is necessary to build a healthy Church.

The Church has faced many challenges throughout history. For example, motivated by Gutenberg's printing press, Western Christianity moved from an oral to a written culture in the Middle Ages. More recently, the Church also had to respond to the Industrial Revolution. Now, digital technology invites the Church to go in new directions. As in the past, significant cultural changes impact the Church's style and practices.

In addressing these new challenges, we follow in the footsteps of those who went before us, as people of hope. In so doing, we must root our lives firmly in the gospel and proclaim it to contemporary people in their language. Making needed changes requires faith, openness, flexibility, wisdom, and discretion, as the Church responds, and the Holy Spirit guides her in the way of truth.

1
CHALLENGES FROM THE DIGITAL WORLD

I discovered the negative impact of our secular, materialistic culture when working with indigenous Native Americans. Over the centuries, they have overcome challenges from alcoholism, pestilence, wars, and oppression, but now, they are losing the battle with our twenty-first century materialism, especially as it influences their youth.

The words of Smiling Raven, a tribal elder, illustrate this influence, when he invited me to view the sunset with him on a beautiful summer evening. As the orange and purple sky disappeared behind the horizon, he said, "Look at that! Before us, we witness a great miracle. As it happens, where are our youth? They're watching television or playing with their cell phones. Technology is winning the day."

Indigenous people are not the only ones challenged by materialism. Many children, teenagers, young adults, and adult Catholics no longer attend Sunday Mass, claiming they are too busy with sporting events, or tired after a lively Saturday night, or have simply left the Church. As materialism takes over, religious practices wane, and secular priorities become the norm. As Jesus said, "No one can serve two masters" (Matt 6:24).

Influences of Contemporary Culture

Through human history, parents taught their children values inherent in their culture through rites of initiation. In so doing, young people learned the deepest dimensions of their culture, including values, a positive style of living, and how to become productive members of society. In other words, they learned the fundamentals of who they were and how to live.

Consequently, children learned their identity and place in society. They picked up a way of living as they engaged with their family, relatives, friends, enemies, and peers. Furthermore, they learned to be faithful to their cultural beliefs and practices.

More recent faith traditions also taught young people fundamental beliefs and practices through similar ways of speaking and acting. Today, traditional rites of passage have broken down, while a digital culture has become a quasi-rite of initiation. The universal scope of the digital media reflects the secularization inherent in technology.

This happens from an early age, for children are intrigued by the computer; they quickly learn computer skills. It's not uncommon to hear a parent say, "If I want to know about a computer or cell phone, I'll ask my child."

The digital world, therefore, not only challenges religious-minded people to identify its pitfalls but also to recognize its values. The future Church needs to interiorize positive values, for when used appropriately, the digital world provides a powerful way to share Jesus's message of salvation.

Positive achievements inherent in technology include developing a cleaner environment, a better standard of living, better global communication, and discovering cures for life-threatening diseases. Artificial intelligence, for example, offers

Challenges from the Digital World

new areas of research and knowledge previously unknown to humanity.

Throughout history, the Church linked the Christian faith with the contemporary oral and written culture. This must now include the digital world. While this presents new opportunities to fashion a better world, it brings new challenges and questions for Catholics.

This happened during the COVID-19 pandemic, when Church attendance, particularly in developed countries, temporarily switched from in-person to online. Such a major change affected Catholic attitudes and practices.

Furthermore, when the long-standing ritual of attending Mass in person was broken, many Catholics felt less inclined to attend. It will take more than a revitalized liturgy or better catechesis to change this attitude.

For some, the convenience of staying home, celebrating Mass digitally and at various times of the day, and choosing different parishes, homilists, and liturgical styles outweighs attending Mass in person.

In addition to the Sunday Mass, communicating on digital videoconferencing platforms became a popular way of holding meetings and teaching children at home instead of in the classroom.

With the increased use of technology in classrooms and other phases of life, education and faith formation took on a new dimension. If today's textbook companies hope to sell their textbooks, they need to include digital resources for classroom use. Lessons taught from books alone are no longer sufficient; increasingly, catechetical instruction uses digital materials.

When ministerial activities are digitized, they need to be complemented by personal communication. What this means for the Church is still to be seen, as technology is employed to conduct meetings, hold conventions, and relate with one another. Digital technology also influences the way parish organizations both locally and nationally communicate and relate to each other.

As the cost of travel increases, such groups must adapt or cease operating. For example, the National Conference of Catechetical Leadership, once the premier organization to further catechetical leadership in the Catholic Church, changed its name and lacks the vibrant energy it once manifested.

MASS COMMUNICATION AND TECHNOLOGY

The digital world intensifies the rapidity of change. "I just can't take it much longer," a friend told me after reflecting on changes at local, national, and global church levels. Technology brings us global information daily. What is newsworthy one day becomes dated a few days later, as more information comes through social media, the Internet, radio, television, and other ways.

On the one hand, mass communication and technology bring blessings, like the ability to get the news from around the world almost as soon as it happens or to receive news from other parts of the world to be near a dying relative.

On the other hand, they also present challenges. The proliferation of data at rapid speeds induces stress and moves us to ask, "What's next?" It causes anger and frustration, as people increasingly do what they want, intensifying frustration and the potential for violence. With such rapid continuous communication, it can be difficult to cope with all that is happening.

Children and teenagers once enjoyed a relatively carefree life and grew up peacefully. Not so anymore. Today's young people are caught in the rat race. They face serious competition in school, are shuffled from home to daycare, and compete in sports, as if they were preparing to be professional athletes. Instead of sporting activities being an enjoyable way to relate with others, many parents and coaches pressure their children to be first.

The rapidity of communication and the proliferation of information go hand in hand. They form the backdrop for how we communicate. In such an environment, there is never enough time for everything. The key is to prioritize what is important.

This fast-paced life has profound consequences for the Church. As it intensifies, we need to learn how to deal with what is happening. Such change includes moving from place to place in search of a job, making our neighborhoods less familiar and unstable; this is particularly true for the younger population. Frequent mobility means that parishes cannot expect the stability of membership that was once the case.

RELATIVISM AND FAITH FORMATION

Throughout history, people recognized norms for what is right or wrong, and good or evil. Over the past hundred years, relativism has changed society and has presented a tremendous challenge for religion.

Influences of Contemporary Culture

Relativism is closely associated with pragmatism. It focuses on the concrete rather than the abstract. It questions absolute truth, as adherents minimize the natural law that defines certain things as right and others as wrong. Relativism, which grew out of academic circles, has spilled over into everyday life, largely through the impact of technology.

Concurrent with those who question unchangeable and objective truths, a relativistic attitude implies that truth itself is relative. It implies that the only truth that makes a difference is your truth.

More than thirty years ago, I witnessed relativistic thinking while teaching in several universities. Even then, during class discussions, it was difficult to get some students to accept the premise that unchangeable truths exist. For them, truth was relative, dependent on cultural norms, their feelings, and what they believed.

Consequently, faith traditions have difficulty convincing people that definite or absolute norms of right and wrong exist and that what is true and false is not subjective, based on cultural norms, one's feelings, personal whims, and fancies. Rather, truth is rooted in the rightness or wrongness of an action itself, as it relates to the bigger picture that traditionally has been associated with the natural law.

A person's view of truth is strongly influenced by his or her culture. In our pragmatic and secular world, it's hard to go against it. With widespread questioning of traditional beliefs on matters like abortion, couples living together outside of marriage, sexual identity, and euthanasia, it is difficult for church leaders and pastoral ministers to convince people that there are absolute or definite moral laws to be followed. This is especially true with young people, where peer pressure and personal feelings often dictate the opposite, especially if moral guidance is not being provided from the Church or their homes.

For many Catholic students of grade- and high-school age, catechetical formation has minimal influence. They rarely attend Sunday Mass or learn about their faith, especially if their parents are not active Catholics. Consequently, there is an increasing trend toward relativism among Catholic youth and adults.

Parish leaders need to be aware of this trend and begin with basic evangelization for people are on their faith journey.

SUBJECTIVE AND OBJECTIVE TRUTH

In his *Summa Theologiae*, St. Thomas Aquinas defines truth as the *adaequatio rei et intellectus* (*ST*, Quest. xvi, art. 1, 3)—the agreement of what is in my mind or spoken to what truly is the case. This description reaffirms what my parents and teachers taught me as a child. Namely, to tell the truth means describing something as it is. To do otherwise deliberately is telling a lie. Religious traditions and society generally regard truth this way.

In one form or another, people instinctively know what truth is. To act otherwise is not being truthful. From ancient times, even civil courts demanded telling the truth and inflicted severe penalties on those who lied or perjured themselves.

With the increase of relativism over the second half of the twentieth century, so too was there an increase in disregard for objective truth. Instead, what is true has become based on a subjective decision.

Influences of Contemporary Culture

This subjective view of truth opens the door to "post-truth." This means that what is described, affirmed, or witnessed is based more on a personal decision about what is the case or what happened, rather than on objective data or facts, and leads to a changing belief that subjective feelings are more important than describing objective events.

This subjective approach, strongly influenced by emotions and often reflected in political thought, leads to an erosion of an objective worldview. Such a perspective is dangerous in that it calls into question basic tenets of society including religious beliefs and traditions.

Truth always had objective and subjective components, but the post-truth movement goes beyond what previous philosophers discussed and ordinary people practiced. It challenges the fiber of social communication.

Parents and parish ministers need to recognize the influence that post-truth has on children and acquaint themselves with it, so they can help their children recognize its presence and learn how to deal with it. Sunday homilies and catechetical sessions can remind parishioners of its ill effects, and through religious instructions, parish leaders are urged to reiterate the absolute need to value objective truth. If this disappears, a basic pillar of society goes with it.

A subjective view of truth sets the foundation for "conspiracy thinking," which occurs when those involved present different views of what happened in a particular instance, even though they may not argue the basic facts of a situation, such as the origin of a pandemic or the outcome of a political election. Often, those who hold to a subjective view of truth disregard basic facts and offer outrageous claims about an event that aligns with their thinking of an individual, social group, or political ideology.

Conspiracy theorists rely on a subjective analysis of what happened when describing a situation with little regard for what is really the case. Conspiracy theories often attempt to change our attitude to a situation or event and can lead to different forms of abuse, be they personal, national, or global, such as blaming a nation or a specific religion for tragedies for which they were not responsible.

Conspiracy theories need to be addressed by church leaders and parishioners need to be assured that the Church remains a harbinger of truth.

THE INTERNET AND PRIVACY

The Internet provides many possibilities for getting important information quickly, but also presents opportunities for deception. Modern technology has made it easier for people to obtain personal information and learn about us and our financial situation. They can steal our savings or even the title of our home from digital information available on the Internet. I almost lost personal information through a clever ruse by a hacker in a foreign country who got into my computer.

It is difficult to maintain the privacy we once enjoyed. When we type our name into an online search engine, it's surprising how much information about our personal and professional life emerges. This situation will only intensify in the future as will our independence as the government and private enterprises learn more about us.

Influences of Contemporary Culture

We pay a price for the speed and efficiency of the computer and Internet. This means that we need to be wise and careful when sharing information and devise ways to maintain our privacy.

As the computer records more of our personal data, including our health and financial records, we begin to realize the profound moral implications. At the same time, the World Wide Web offers new ways for us to be missionary disciples. When donating to charitable causes, we need to be prudent to avoid bogus groups seeking donations to satisfy themselves. Being computer savvy means being wise to fraud and manipulation.

Such manipulation also includes those who take advantage of children and adults through immoral and immodest efforts to lead them into dishonorable pursuits. For this reason, a parent needs to know how to use a cell phone and the Internet, lest their children be led into immoral actions.

Privacy is a blessing, a truth I realize while sitting on my farmhouse porch in Indiana. When watching news broadcasts of what is happening, however, I wonder how many cameras exist today. They seem to be everywhere! Ordinary citizens have become our press photographers, as they take camera shots of mass shootings or minor accidents. This lack of privacy causes me to ask how far it will go.

Although we don't want to be paranoid by conspiracy thinking, we wonder how much information the government and businesses have on us that is learned from our computers, cell phones, and other devices.

What does this lack of privacy mean for the future? How can we maintain privacy in a technologically dominated society? This requires a new way of thinking and acting, including an important place for the cell phone as an essential ingredient

Challenges from the Digital World

for life in the twenty-first century. We depend on it for communication, safety, and organizing our lives. It serves us well when something happens. In saying this, we recognize that the cell phone is already useful for medical, safety, and communication aspects of life. In time, it will afford endless new uses, including for the Church.

When reflecting on the growing significance of digital technology, the issue of artificial intelligence often arises. Artificial intelligence is the ability of machines to carry out actions that usually require human reasoning such as playing chess, identifying speech recognition, or self-driving vehicles. It affords tremendous opportunities for developments in science, medicine, economics, and other fields. At the same time, it is fraught with danger.

Digital computers and artificial intelligence must be considered from an ethical viewpoint. Their limits and interaction with humans are major concerns of society, generally, and the Church, in particular. The Church must continually ascertain what is positive and morally permissible and what is destructive and threatening to humanity and unethical. Just because something can be produced is no reason to make it. The common good of humanity must be kept in mind.

Sound ethical thinking will help us determine the moral use and limits of technological developments as we learn new and better ways to live.

FOR DISCUSSION

1. Why do we need to keep up with the developments in digital technology?

Influences of Contemporary Culture

2. How can parents take the lead in spiritualizing this technological culture by helping their children recognize the moral values of technology and avoid its pitfalls?

3. With constant change, why does it become increasingly important to prioritize what is really important in our daily lives?

4. Why is it important to say no to what is of less importance and to recognize that such a response may be a gift of the Holy Spirit?

5. How do the fundamentals of Catholicism help us and our children respond to the growing sense of relativism in society?

6. Why does truth need to be rooted in objective norms and an objective worldview?

7. How can parents and teachers help children cultivate an objective view of truth and teach them the skills to form their consciences.

2

CHANGING PERSPECTIVES IN A TROUBLED WORLD

As digital technology becomes more prominent, our lives have to adapt and change, which has implications for our faith. This chapter considers such changes and how the Church can respond to their implications, such as gun violence, anger, tension, and dissent in society.

GUN VIOLENCE

Evidence of gun violence has intensified in recent years. We only need to observe what is reported in the media. Violence has existed from the beginning of humankind, but it has become more noticeable in recent times.

During my college years, I worked in my father's store. One beautiful afternoon, a woman ran into the store and cried out, "Hide, there's a gunfight in the street." We ducked behind the counter until the shooting stopped.

Influences of Contemporary Culture

Two men just robbed the store across the street, but unknownst to them, the handicapped store owner had a gun by the cash register. As they hit him, he fell, picked up his gun, and shot both in their legs, intending to stop them but not take their lives.

After the shooting ended, I went outside and saw a trail of blood going around his store and into the alley. It disappeared at the back door of an apartment house. Seeing the blood, I became apprehensive, because later that day, I had to make deliveries near the house where the trail of blood ended. Initially, the robbers hid there, but they soon needed medical attention and surrendered.

This event has been the closest I came to witnessing an actual shooting. Seventy years later, I remember the emotional toll that it had on me and those in my neighborhood. The storekeeper was so disturbed that shortly after this happened, he closed his small store that had been sustaining him in his retirement.

It would be true to say that the climate of urban and rural cities in the United States has become more violent than those days when I worked in my father's store.

The proliferation of guns has affected the way people cope with their emotions, especially anger. When I was young, my peers and neighbors sometimes disagreed, and it was not unusual for a crowd to gather around those who were arguing. If a fight broke out, it usually lasted a few minutes until one of them gave up, ran away, or an adult stepped in to stop the fight.

Today, if a fight breaks out at school or in the neighborhood, it is not uncommon for combatants to pull out guns and start shooting. We witness the devastating effects wrought by such shootings, but seem powerless to deal with the physical, emotional, and personal ramifications of such violence.

When I was young, guns were severely restricted. Gradually, laws changed, and more guns appeared as did the violence and the number of families being ripped apart. The immorality and sinfulness of gun violence must be addressed in sermons and catechetical sessions. This means considering gun violence from more than a shooting perspective. Such shootings are sinful and violate God's commandment, "Thou shall not kill." We need to view such moral issues from the perspective of human dignity, not merely as violent actions in a secular world.

Anger is nothing new, but the inability to cope effectively with anger leads to uncontrolled violence. Anger is an important emotion in our life, especially when things do not go as we hoped, we feel left out, or someone violates our space. We need to know how to control it. Classic examples of anger often happen while driving a car—when a driver makes a U-turn in front of us or goes through a red light while frustrated with the movement of traffic.

Today, practically no area of the country is immune from guns and mass shootings. What will it be like in twenty years, when the number of firearms continues to increase along with the anger that motivates our response to situations? Is this the legacy that we want to leave our future generations?

Our civic leaders seem powerless to curb the violence, but unless guns are severely restricted little change can happen. Church leaders need to speak out against violence of all kinds and its accompanying anger in the spirit of Jesus, the Prince of Peace.

Influences of Contemporary Culture

Gun violence is a good entry point for parents to catechize their children about possessing and using guns. They can stress the dignity of life and how shooting someone not only violates that person but goes against the commandment of God to love one another.

Any discussion about gun violence must include the larger picture regarding our respect for life. The challenge to respect life is complex. For example, we see the outpouring of sympathy when a mass shooting occurs but lack the resolve to do much about the situation. We see it also in the way citizens help victims of natural disasters such as tornadoes or floods.

When the Supreme Court overthrew *Roe v. Wade*, we witnessed an outpouring of anger from those who refused to affirm the right to life of babies in their mother's womb, as if they were not human and deserving of life.

When teaching the next generation about the dignity of all human life, we pray that the Church's message of human dignity be heard, as the children of today grow into maturity. It is vital for them to understand that the sacredness of life extends from a person's conception to one's last breath, regardless of age, background, or race.

Today, the way many people deal with anger leads to more violence and tragedy. The lack of parental guidance, free access to guns, an overriding climate of frustration, and little accountability have led to the surge of violence, often caused by uncontrolled anger.

A classic example of communal anger and violence occurred on January 6, 2022, when a mob attacked the Capitol building in Washington. Regardless of one's political leaning, it's necessary to remain firm in our Christian beliefs as we strive to regain trust in the media and our civic leaders. Since faith is influenced by the culture around us, skepticism regarding civic matters influences how we trust any leader.

Trust in today's church leaders has been jeopardized by the lack of trust in society generally, but also in the failure of some church leaders to take appropriate action in the sex abuse scandal and other pastoral matters. As a result, church leaders do not get the automatic trust of the Catholic population. Instead, they need to earn it. In other words, bishops, priests, religious, and lay ecclesial ministers need to earn the trust of those they serve. The future church will be strongly influenced by how Catholic leaders respond to Jesus's call to humbly serve the whole body of believers.

UNITY, DISSENT, AND TENSION

On a bleak Sunday afternoon in December 1941, my family drove to the "Glass Barn" in Cincinnati. I was seven years old. While sitting in the parking lot, we heard the news report on the radio that "the Japanese have attacked Pearl Harbor."

This shocking headline announced the beginning of the United States' involvement in the Second World War. Immediately, we witnessed a unified effort throughout the country to overcome the aggressors and defend ourselves from attack. One aspect of the war effort will forever remain embedded in my heart. It was the collaborative response of Americans everywhere, working as a fine-tuned machine, to achieve victory. This included a response to the war effort and a tremendous revival of faith, as our country turned to God. What our citizens accomplished together in four years was nothing short of miraculous. I have never seen a more united America.

Influences of Contemporary Culture

This unity continued through the Korean War, but by the 1960s, rumblings of dissent had begun to surface, as our unity as a people gradually split. Many factors were involved, including the Civil Rights Movement that sought to give African Americans their rights, the role of America in the Vietnam War, and the women's rights for equality.

During this period, dissent emerged within the Church. Catholics manifested disagreement with the Church on matters such as birth control, vernacular liturgies, and other reforms initiated by the Second Vatican Council. These conflicts included conflicts over liturgy and how to teach religious education.

During these changing times, one specific issue in the Church, birth control, caused deep conflict. Pope St. Paul VI's encyclical, *Humanae vitae*, enflamed major disagreement throughout the Catholic population regarding the morality of artificial contraception. This encyclical set the groundwork for current differences between Catholics today.

While the birth control controversy continued, the fight around abortion came to the forefront. Church teaching and civil legislation clashed with the 1973 Supreme Court decision regarding *Roe v. Wade*, which legalized abortion on a national level. It remained in effect until the Supreme Court overturned the decision with *Dobbs v. Jackson* on June 24, 2022.

The Church's teaching on abortion is that from the first moment of conception, the fertilized embryo is a human being and may not be killed or artificially aborted.

In addition to these issues, the sex abuse scandal, brought to light in the 1980s, evoked a strong response from Catholics. It resulted in lost confidence in Church authority, the defection of many parishioners, and a focus on the Church's dealing with children and youth. Current Church policies address how to employ safe practices when dealing with young people and safeguarding children.

The divisions in civil and Church society have led to a divided nation and a divided Church. Conflicting opinions need to be addressed to ensure the future vitality of civic and Church society.

THE PANDEMIC

When I was a boy, civic, church, and military leaders seemed bigger than life. We never dreamed that we would see a president, pope, or war hero, like Douglas McArthur. We admired and held them in great respect, accepted their authority, and followed their directives.

This changed in the 1960s through the widespread use of television, the growth of rapid transportation, the Vietnam War, and other factors. The questioning of Church authorities also increased during this time following the Second Vatican Council. Overall, this era led to doubt and skepticism about the future.

Vulnerable people look for leaders to bring them out of their difficulties and set new directions. When drastic change occurs, unrest follows, as it did with the onslaught of the 2019 coronavirus pandemic. In civic and Church matters, Catholics looked for leaders and found few to give them solid direction. Everyone seemed vulnerable, and no one knew how to alleviate the fear and panic, the unrest, anger, sickness, death, and suffering that accompanied the pandemic.

The pandemic accentuated the need for civic and church leaders. Politicians hesitated to rock the boat, afraid of losing

Influences of Contemporary Culture

votes. Church leaders said little. Business leaders feared for corporate profits, and that loss of political clout would ensue. Those in charge tried different things with little success.

Different opinions abounded about closing businesses, keeping churches open, developing vaccines, avoiding family members, friends, and so on. People feared for their lives and decided between conflicting opinions about what to do. Leaders who did come forth often were judged harshly. Anger that had built up over the past fifty years surfaced and unleashed an increased violence in many men and women.

While many awaited vaccines to protect us, some people became skeptical about their safety. Some got vaccinated, others refused. The pandemic highlighted our inherent individualism while the common good took a back seat.

The pandemic changed our country drastically. What remained included skepticism, fear of reoccurrence, anger, violence, questioning leadership, changing business patterns, and a host of other issues.

For the Church, restrictions on attending Sunday Mass during the pandemic resulted in a decrease in Mass attendance and the need to refocus Church loyalty. Some Catholics returned to Church, others did not.

For children and youth, the pandemic robbed them of weekly catechetical instruction, and regular church attendance. It has been difficult for them to regain their lost years of religious formation, especially if they received little or no faith learning in their homes or parishes. Many families have stopped coming to church entirely. How this will affect the future generation as they enter adulthood is yet to be determined.

While acknowledging the negative consequences of the

pandemic, we also need to celebrate the positive results and refocus unhealthy attitudes and actions that developed during those times. It's up to each one of us to reflect on this issue and decide what we will pass on to future generations from the experience of this pandemic.

FOR DISCUSSION

We now reflect on the current situation and the challenges in passing on the faith.

1. What does the increase in anger and gun violence indicate about our understanding of human life?

2. What does compassion shown to the relatives and friends of victims of violence indicate about our society?

3. How can we legitimately deal with anger in our own life and community?

4. What different emotions did the pandemic trigger in you and your family? How did you deal with these emotions?

5. How can we encourage the next generation to deal positively with negative emotions?

6. What are the greatest challenges in keeping young people active and involved in today's church community?

3

NEW WORLD POSSIBILITIES

In this chapter, we focus on the environment and the ramifications caused by the developments in technology. We consider both the new possibilities and challenges as we reflect on financial stress, ecology, and ethnic refocusing.

FINANCIAL STRESS

Recently, a television commercial depicted a man who wanted to be the first person on earth to live until he was 125 years old. A century ago, it would have been amazing for a person to live to be 100 years old. Today, however, it is bold to predict the limits of a human being's lifespan. And yet, medical advances that add to our overall health, lifespan, and well-being now face challenges arising from the environment and cultural divisions in the United States.

The rapid pace of society affects every phase of life. Increasingly, it strains our economy, and, unless we temper our spending, the value of our currency will continue to decline and cause added stress.

New World Possibilities

To illustrate the differences in the value of our currency, I am reminded of a family vacation to Quebec, Canada, when I was in high school. My parents budgeted ten dollars a day for our evening meals. This amount was sufficient for six of us to eat dinner in restaurants. Today, the same meals would cost at least ten times that much.

To illustrate further how prices have risen, in 1968, a person could pay just over a hundred dollars per acre for abandoned farmland in Indiana. Now, the annual property taxes are at least half that amount.

We are likely to spend more in the future than we do today. Money will have less value and products will cost more. This has significant implications for our well-being. Who knows how long Social Security funds will last or whether the government will subsidize those in need and offer them health care! It is becoming more costly to pay for research efforts to improve our health, run our economy, repair our nation's infrastructure, support our military, travel into outer space, and so on.

Such monetary demands challenge us, not only financially, but also emotionally and spiritually. Lack of money creates family tension, when our income is not sufficient to provide for sustainable housing and the necessities of life.

At the same time, increased costs stretch some parishes to the limits, as they strive to pay just wages to employees and maintain church property, buildings, and other expenses. The decline in church membership along with the closing and merging of parishes causes us to question where such resources will be found.

Living longer brings greater concern in caring for the elderly as well as providing for growing children. Consequently, some families who are currently raising and educating their children are also caring for older relatives.

THE ENVIRONMENT

In the Book of Genesis, God blessed Adam and Eve and told them to "Be fruitful and multiply, and fill the earth and subdue it; and have dominion over...every living thing that moves upon the earth" (Gen 1:28).

This responsibility is incumbent on every human being. Most Indigenous people realize their obligation as stewards of the earth. Native tribes in Alaska and other countries accept the goods of the earth as gifts from the creator. In return, they pledge not to waste anything but to take from Mother Earth only what they need. They express their thanks for what other earth creatures give them by way of food, hides, and items from which they make clothes or use for other pursuits.

With the coming of technology, people increasingly abused this trust. Stewardship became manipulation rather than respect for the beauty and utility that nature provides.

I witnessed such disregard for creation while traveling through the Rocky Mountains. As we meandered through a mountainous region, the road snaked along a ledge toward a deep valley surrounded by two beautiful mountains. Flowers, grass, majestic forests, clear skies, and silk clouds clothed the landscape.

As we drove around a sharp bend, our basking in the beautiful place changed. Before us on the right, we saw that the top of the mountain had been removed by large earth-moving vehicles. There, we witnessed a huge, ugly brown and black level spot, dug out where the summit of the mountain

New World Possibilities

once stood. This section of the mountain was strip-mined for coal, uranium, copper, and other minerals. This horrible abuse of a once beautiful land became permanently imprinted in my memory as a testament to how we as humans can destroy our natural resources.

A few years later, I experienced a similar abuse when observing a massive spill of polluted water and dead fish in the ocean, the result of discarded plastic items and oil spills. Such events demonstrated firsthand what happens if we do not preserve planet Earth.

It's consoling to witness the strong rection of the younger generation to such environmental manipulation. We need to support their commitment to correct it. Preserving natural resources is a blessed goal. We are obliged to carry out God's injunction to steward the earth in a responsible way. If future generations are to succeed in their responsibility, they will need our support.

As we care for our planet, we look beyond it into space. Many countries on earth are exploring the outer recesses of the universe. Space travel is still in its infancy, but advances in digital and other technologies are making it more accessible and available.

In early Christian times, the earth was considered the center of the universe. Christians believed that Jesus came to earth to redeem its inhabitants and the entire universe from sin and punishment. Copernicus (1473–1543) taught that the sun, not the earth, is the center of our universe. This issued a revolution in thought and changed our perspective on the universe.

From the fifteenth century, scientists came to realize that the sun is a small star in comparison with the other stars in the universe, and that the earth was swimming in vast regions of

Influences of Contemporary Culture

space. This brought about a change in thinking about Jesus as our redeemer. Even today, theologians ask if he only atoned for the sins of humans on earth or whether his redemption extended to the entire universe and to creatures who might live in other galaxies.

In our era of increased space travel, we wonder if other rational creatures live beyond planet Earth. Since Earth is a small fragment of what exists in space, it is reasonable to conclude that other intelligent creatures live somewhere else, perhaps in a vastly different way than us. We ask the same questions as earlier theologians: Does the salvation offered by Jesus extend to them and are they also in need of redemption?

Right now, these questions are merely speculative. Someday, however, they may be real. With new, yet unknown ways of communicating technologically, we need to prepare coming generations to be open to whatever may come. We do so by focusing on matters of faith in such a new world, where issues raised through exploration beyond this planet open us to other views of our universe.

Belief in Jesus as our redeemer and in the Church as a body of believers will last until the end of time, assisting us both on our journey on earth and to eternal life. As we make our journey, God enjoins us to protect and be stewards of the environment.

The "Green Revolution" addresses issues dealing with pollution and the weakening of the ozone layer that protects Earth from the harmful rays of the sun. Ecologists offer many suggestions, but we need to be careful that substituting one thing for another doesn't make matters worse.

Making the world a safer place and removing harmful contaminants from the air is a laudable task. While working in my father's store in my youth, we had one source of heat in the winter—an old potbelly furnace. By day's end, black mucus from coal dust settled in my throat and nose. My parched and dry throat took a couple of days to clear up. Working in a part of town where coal belched from factory chimneys near the store only intensified the soot and added to my problems in my throat and nose.

I was delighted when we got a gas furnace at home. It was much cleaner. Today, with the push to eliminate coal and natural gas and move to solar and wind energy, we witness a new revolution and ask the question, What are the advantages of the changes we make to improve and serve the common good?

Considering the consequences of major changes, I recall the miles of windmills to produce energy while driving through the Midwest. After seeing them, I learned that they have a twenty-five-year lifespan. No one has adequately answered what happens to the windmills when they become obsolete. Will they become a massive junk heap?

Consider what happens to plastic straws and cups, and other discarded items that now form a floating island in the Pacific Ocean. How can we ensure that when we adopt a new form of energy, that what we discard in the future is not toxic to the environment?

Electric cars are becoming more common. It is not our intention to argue for or against them, but to indicate that what is done must serve the long-term common good and not just satisfy what is beneficial at present.

While we develop a better world through technology, we must consider the consequences of the changes we make. While this has been necessary in the past, it is more imperative

Influences of Contemporary Culture

that what is done today happens ethically for our own well-being and that of the planet.

As the earth evolves, plants and animals have utilized waste and adapted to natural events like earthquakes and volcanoes. While God gave humans stewardship of the earth, inanimate nature can no longer cope with excessive waste, the rapid destruction of forests, or the pollution of streams. Humans need to assist in this effort. We need to accept our ethical obligation to steward the earth in responsible ways. This means taking care of and protecting the rights of others, especially in dealing with the moral issues we discussed in the last chapter.

Preserving the dignity of humanity also means avoiding war at all costs. We will always have the potential for war, but Christians must go out of their way to avoid it.

In the 1950s, my high school classmates were drafted into the Korean War. Then, in the 1960s, the Vietnam War broke out. As the years passed, strife continued in Kuwait, Iraq, and around the globe. In February 2022, Russia invaded Ukraine. The scenario continues, with the threat of nuclear warfare in the background. Wars will continue while nations seek more power, territory, and dominance over others.

Most nations prefer peace, but some nations will always seek to conquer and grow in power. How will our present legacy of war affect future generations? We can rest assured that they will face it, even though humans desire to overcome evil and live in peace. How can we prepare them?

Following in the way of Jesus gives us a solid starting point to strive for peace. He stresses the value of human life and that taking what belongs to others is wrong, regardless of whether it is stealing a candy bar in a store, padding the books

New World Possibilities

in business affairs, or taking another's life in war. No country has the right to invade the sovereignty of another.

Near my house, there is a nuclear bomb shelter from the Vietnam War era. It serves as a stern reminder of the tragedy of war and that no one can justify the killing of another. This symbol from the past reminds us of the immorality of warfare along with our desire to preserve the planet.

Striving for peace sets the stage for a better understanding that the only way to find meaning in this world is to treat our neighbors as we want to be treated. Working for peace affords us the opportunity to encourage our youth to live by the tenets of their faith and to become active in their parishes, school faith communities, and institutions of higher learning.

The growth of atheism in our troubled society reminds us to turn to God in prayer and adoration. If ever we needed the wisdom of the Holy Spirit, it is today. A worthwhile question to ask is: How can we grow in our faith?

MORAL AND ETHICAL TEACHING

We are ethical creatures and something within us informs us what is right and wrong. We call this inner voice our "conscience." Through human history, the culture where people lived set the norms for them to follow.

The basic tenets of different civilizations are similar. This is because a universal natural law guides humans, leading them to establish basic beliefs and modes of conduct. Since this natural law has a common source in God, similar designs are reflected in nature and human civilizations.

Influences of Contemporary Culture

In the Judeo-Christian tradition, the basic tenets of right and wrong are found in the Ten Commandments. They are the foundation for Western civilization and are followed by Jews, Christians, and many others.

When I was a child, my parents and teachers taught me the basic norms of right conduct from the *Baltimore Catechism*. Our Catholic school teachers had us memorize these foundations of our faith and applied them to right moral conduct. They were clear and precise, and by the time we reached eighth grade, these fundamentals were firmly rooted in our minds and hearts.

In the 1960s, as society became more complex, the Church saw the need to address these basic tenets of faith. This happened initially at the Second Vatican Council and led to a fuller explanation of Catholic beliefs and practices. The Council addressed the complexities of our emerging society and refocused our discussion of issues such as the morality of nuclear warfare, ecological concerns, freedom of expression, and more. In so doing, the Council shifted Catholic teaching and practices into a modern context to address the various challenges of secular society.

Today, it has become progressively more important that Catholic parents are well-versed in Catholic teaching. They benefit greatly if they learn what is happening in the Church and commit themselves to provide sound moral teaching to their children.

Basic Catholic moral and ethical teaching has not changed, but the secular world presents great challenges to accept the Church's teachings, because of the worldly approach that it offers to children and youth. To counter the impact of materialistic culture, it is important for parents to guide their children to deal correctly with social media and society. This is a vital aspect of good Catholic parenting.

FOR DISCUSSION

We now reflect on current new issues and the challenges in passing on the faith.

1. What are some challenges of living a long life for future generations of churchgoers?

2. How might growing inflation impact your future and that of your loved ones? What can you do about it?

3. How might further exploration of the universe and the possibility of other forms of life enhance or challenge the faith of future generations?

4. How does the possibility of superior forms of life existing beyond our solar system affect your view of God, the Church, and living a life of prayer?

5. Based on your own experience, is the issue of controlling waste and pollution vital for the future preservation of the planet and our own well-being?

6. Why is being responsible stewards in caring for the earth a moral obligation of every Christian?

7. What advice would you give to a young parent who wants to raise their children in the Catholic faith?

Part II
Changes in the Church and Society

The social, religious, and materialistic changes described in part 1 significantly impact the future of the Church. This second part offers theological and pastoral insights to address the changes and their impact on Catholicism.

The challenges facing the Church are many and varied. Many of them stem from the Church sex abuse scandal and issues related to the pandemic, and consequently, many Catholics are leaving the Church. The Church must face these challenges if it wants to have a vibrant future.

Many devoted Catholics want to know how the Church can stem the tide of people leaving her and continue to carry out Jesus's mission. To address these issues, the Church needs to proclaim Jesus's message, exercise new leadership, and address internal divisions.

The Changing Face of Catholicism

In the United States, the Catholic population varies in ethnicity, age, and according to whether they hold traditional or progressive perspectives. Despite this variety, the Church is rooted in basic beliefs and practices, outlined in the *Catechism of the Catholic Church* and through the Church's liturgical rites.

Challenges within the Church make it difficult for some Catholics to remain or educate their children in the faith. This difficulty often springs from lack of trust, a prerequisite for any vibrant parish. On the one hand, if parishes try to reach their members through meetings, sporting activities, and so on, they usually have minimal success. On the other hand, if they welcome people where they are on their life journey, regardless of their financial position, their age, or sexuality, and help them connect with the faith, they have some success in connecting with people's deeper needs.

Where can parishes begin this connection? The answer is found in the cross of Christ and not in the cell phone. The early Church preached the crucified and risen Christ. He is the answer to secularism, symbolized by the cell phone advertisement on the six-story building mentioned in part 1. The cell phone stands in sharp contrast to the common practice of hanging a crucifix in Catholic homes.

In our home, the crucifix was the first thing we saw when we entered the front door. It reminded us that family life centered around the cross of Christ and all that implies. As simple as it seems, this message came from the early disciples, who preached the crucified and risen Christ and converted the world. Jesus's message was folly to the power brokers of his time. But for those who accepted it with an open heart, it became the key to understanding that only faith can address the deeper search of the human person. To the wise of the world, the cross is as irrelevant as the poor whom Jesus came to save. To those who accept its message, however, Jesus promises happiness and eternal life.

How is Christ's message different from the secular message of today? The latter considers poverty as failure and affluence as success. Nonbelievers do not recognize that after the sin of Adam and Eve, poverty is the constant reminder that what the world proclaims as important cannot be the answer.

If we live by the message of Christ crucified, however, we are moved beyond the physical poverty of health, the psychological poverty of a troubled heart, the spiritual poverty of being bound to riches, and the economic poverty of a person unable to break its bonds.

The Church's goal is to teach the world that the values of Christ transform society. In so doing, life becomes whole and holy, as we strive toward eternal blessedness with God for all eternity. This is the message to those coming after us.

For many, the Church has lost its attraction, primarily because of the impact of secular culture outlined in the previous part. So we must ask: What can be done to strengthen the life and vitality of the Church?

This second part suggests new directions for Catholics to follow in the ever-shifting digital world. Those who accept the challenge to proclaim the good news, will include the wealthy and poor, the well-educated and those not well versed in the Church's teaching. Regardless of their socioeconomic condition, they need a new awareness of what it means to be Church.

This awareness requires a strong focus on the family, the most basic unit of the Church. Families are domestic churches, committed to following the Lord in a new era

Changes in the Church and Society

of evangelization. Each must be aware of the obstacles and opportunities that they face. In accepting this call to reenergize their wounded Church in an ever-changing technological world, they also need to recognize the pitfalls they face. To embrace their calling, we offer suggestions for tomorrow's Catholics living in a digital world.

4

FAMILY, THE PEOPLE OF GOD, AND COMMUNITY

To communicate Christ's message and that of the Church in a twenty-first century digital culture, we begin by considering three aspects that sustain the future of Catholicism. These three aspects are the family, the people of God, and a sense of community.

FAMILY

The family is the key to a vibrant, changing church. It is within the family that we first learn of God's love, of Jesus coming to live among us, and of his real presence in the Eucharist. Our relationship with God and with the Church is deeply affected by our beliefs and practices that are formed within the family.

When I was a small boy, I would sit with my grandmother as she told me stories of her family leaving Holland and coming to live in the United States. Her family was poor, so on

Changes in the Church and Society

their voyage here they slept in the bottom of the ship with the animals, cargo, and luggage.

She told me of one big storm that threatened to sink the ship. To prevent this from happening, they were ordered to throw much of what they had brought with them into the ocean. I sensed her sorrow as she described throwing overboard their most prized possession, namely, a large statue of the Blessed Virgin Mary.

As a child, I wondered why this was so important to her. As an adult, I realized that it symbolized the faith of her family and the challenges that their faith had endured. For grandma, the statue represented what was important in life, especially the need to maintain their family's Catholic faith in the new world. Her commitment to her faith had a profound effect on our family, as it does whenever faith is a priority in the home.

The future of Catholicism is strongly affected by the environment of today's families. While it was once generally presumed that Catholic families practiced their faith and attended Mass on Sundays, this is no longer the case. Consequently, it is vitally important that parents, from the beginning of their marriage, intentionally strive to foster a faith-centered family that will help them counter the negative influences of secularism.

I am reminded of Charles, a descendant of a pioneering family that settled in central Kentucky after the Revolutionary War. Charles is a Catholic, who can trace his ancestry to a Catholic family that first came from Maryland. While visiting his home recently, he showed me a small catechism-like book that was printed in the early 1800s and written by a missionary priest who came to Kentucky several times a year to minister to the Catholic families who had settled there. The priest gave copies of books like this to Catholic mothers to catechize their families who had settled west of the Appalachian Mountains.

The mothers used these books to teach their children the basics of the faith and prepare them for receiving the sacraments, which the priest administered when he visited their settlements. In this way, the faith was preserved and thrived in these wilderness regions until permanent parishes were established and priests could be assigned to minister to those Catholics living there.

In a sense, we live in a wilderness today—not so much a rural wilderness but a secular wilderness—where faith is challenged. In our secular wilderness, with fewer priests and religious women, parents must foster the faith of their families, like those early pioneering mothers and ancestors of Charles in central Kentucky.

Today, the situation and challenges of faith have changed. Within this digital world, we need to strengthen the image that young boys and girls have of themselves despite their many material possessions.

Often, a poor self-image can be influenced by the conflicting messages that young people receive from social media, including at times the bullying they receive and other negative personal encounters. A person's self-image needs to be connected to their faith, beginning with God's love of them and their realization that God made every person in God's own image. This gives children great dignity and lays the foundation for who they really are—their self-worth. Such positive messages help young people to put into perspective the many conflicting images and messages they receive from social media.

From both theological and ecclesial perspectives, a fundamental requirement for the future vibrancy of Catholicism

Changes in the Church and Society

is the important focus on the family. This means that from the beginning of a marriage, faith must be central to the life of the family. To accomplish this requires regular prayer, good example, and sound teaching about God, Jesus, Mary, and other great heroes of the faith.

When families grow up without seeing their parents go to church, praying, or discussing matters of faith at home, the focus of faith is lost. This absence of faith is a real challenge coming from within the Church, for family faith formation is at the heart of Jesus's call to evangelize. We cannot have a revitalized Church unless the family is an integral part of it.

If there is little or no prayer in the family, few conversations about the faith, and parents who seldom attend Sunday Mass, many young people will not practice their faith! A parish needs to enkindle the faith in parishioners when little is happening in their homes to motivate family members.

Now, there is no simple answer to why Catholic youth, whose parents are faithful Catholics, do not practice their faith. In this regard, Catholic parents often throw up their hands in frustration, saying they cannot force their children to go to Sunday Mass without turning them off completely. Similarly, the blame cannot be put on the poor quality of catechetical books. I've been involved in the publication of Catholic books for elementary and secondary grades for years. In my role, I know the strict demands of the Bishops' Committee on the Catechism, required for their approval of books to be used in Catholic parishes and schools. Regardless, the number of Catholic youth and young adults leaving the faith continues to grow.

Nonetheless, we need to ask: What does this say about ministry to youth? As a starting point, it demands that we welcome students where they are and go from there, not by

Family, the People of God, and Community

focusing on memorizing the truths of the faith or passing an examination. Rather, catechizing children must help them form their consciences correctly and learn to distinguish between what is right and wrong. For this to happen, parents and catechists need practical examples to teach students the fundamentals of the faith and the limitations of secular society, the social media, and relativism.

Most importantly, faith formation begins in the home, where children see their parents practicing their faith. This is enhanced when their peers support them and are examples of Christian living.

Change needs to begin with increased parish efforts to catechize families and to help them see that youth receive the greatest incentive to grow in faith in their domestic church or church of the home.

Parishes can support families by recommending value-centered programs on the Internet, religious news, books, and using technology to increase their knowledge of the faith. Diocesan offices and Catholic publishers can take the lead in showing how this is done. Parishes can assist parents by addressing the positive and negative influences of cell phones and the Internet—suggesting good programs and questioning objectionable ones.

Given the hectic pace of life today, parents are barely able to get through their own day, let alone engage in their children's religious formation. Many do not know where to begin and have limited knowledge of what the Church teaches. Overwhelmed, they do little to assist their children with matters of faith, besides showing them love and a good example.

Well-minded parents, who often do little more to supplement what their children learn in religion classes, feel that they have met their responsibility for their children's faith formation. In fact, it should be the opposite. Namely, what children learn in parish catechetical classes should supplement the grounding in faith that they experience at home. The need to focus on the family as a domestic church is increasing as parishes consolidate and the number of priests, religious, well-trained catechists, and religion teachers declines.

Finally, for the faith within families to be revitalized, parish leaders and parishioners must be more concerned about supporting and fostering this faith than about parish finances or organization. It means that priests and deacons must preach about the effectiveness of family faith and demonstrate its priorities within vibrant parish communities.

THE PEOPLE OF GOD

After reflecting on the role of the family, we now consider the Church as the people of God. Vatican II used this expression, preferring it to a more hierarchical image. It received strong affirmation in the Dogmatic Constitution on the Church, *Lumen gentium*.

When debating the preparatory materials for the Council, the bishops settled on the idea of the Church as mystery. They then considered the image of the Church as the people of God, and finally they addressed the hierarchy. This order demonstrated a move from an ecclesiology centered on Holy Orders to one that was grounded in the community through baptism, changing the tenor of the Church from a clerical to a people-centered one—one that is centered on community.

As a biblical term, the "people of God" refers to the

Family, the People of God, and Community

Jewish nation in the Old Testament. God called the Hebrew nation to be his people, and He was their God. When Jesus established his Church, Christians became the new people of God.

Since the Second Vatican Council, the Catholic Church has undergone significant changes. A revitalized Church needs a faith community that is united. In so doing, the challenges that the early Church faced at Corinth after Pentecost give us insights on how to proceed.

Corinth was a city with merchants and traders coming from various parts of the Roman Empire. Its secularized nature was indicative of today's materialistic world, and St. Paul struggled to maintain the vibrancy of the faith.

In his First Letter to the Corinthians, St. Paul stresses the Christian call to holiness in the pagan world where Christians lived, emphasizing that God gave them the necessary grace to remain faithful. He writes of their spiritual gifts that would enable them to endure suffering and even death for the sake of the kingdom of God (cf. 1 Cor 1:1–9). In a subsequent letter to the community at Corinth, Paul upbraided them for their failures, but only after supporting them and challenging them to remain true to the life that Christ had given them (cf. 2 Cor 2ff.).

With the growth of secularism today, St. Paul's words remind us that, for the Church to grow and thrive, we must focus on spiritual rebirth, recognize our call to holiness, ask for God's grace, and utilize our spiritual talents.

The Second Vatican Council stressed community, the role of the laity, and our dignity received at baptism. In so doing, the community of believers assumed a new role in salvation, receiving fresh initiatives and ways to minister.

Changes in the Church and Society

Before Vatican II, the laity played a minor role in church leadership, which was mostly exercised by bishops and priests. Even religious women, influential in establishing Catholic schools in the United States, had little responsibility for Church governance.

Organizational change does not come easily, neither do changing attitudes toward liturgy, social ministry, and other aspects of Church life. When the Council focused on the people of God and the Church as a community, it opened the doors for the laity to exercise new roles in church leadership, but it reserved ordained priestly ministry to celibate men. Married men, however, could be ordained to the diaconate.

Changing views on Church governance continue to be a source of conflict, illustrated in the initial response to the call to synodality, initiated by Pope Francis. In this process, Catholics raised questions about ordaining married men as priests and about new leadership roles for women. In the future, these issues will continue to challenge the Church, as will ministry to the LGBTQ community and other moral lifestyle issues.

Many Catholics favor an open resolution of such issues, while others push for maintaining current Church practice. In this discussion, differences between the hierarchy and laity and conflicting attitudes within the Church need to be addressed openly and with respect for those involved.

Mutual communication between clergy and laity is important. The entire community of believers is responsible for the well-being of the Church, and it is the right and responsibility of all the baptized to further Christ's mission. Pope Francis reminds us that a new clericalism is emerging, bringing tension into the body of believers. Unless the clergy's role is focused on the whole community of the baptized, using the model of servant leadership, the future will not portend well for Catholicism.

The relationship between the clergy and laity must involve the role of women in the community of the faithful. This issue is of vital importance in "being church." The quest for equality causes many women to leave the Church. Although significant strides have been made to involve women in different aspects of Church, much more is still needed.

VIBRANT COMMUNITIES

A community is a group of people who care about one another, making sacrifices for its members and making their welfare a top priority. The first experience of a community is often the family. We learn what it means to be a community not from textbooks or teachers but from our experience of living together as a family. A loving family puts the needs of one another first.

In addition to the family, we identify church groups, such as religious orders of men and women, Catholic schools, and parishes, as faith communities.

Institutions differ from communities in that they provide organizational structures that enable its members to work efficiently to fulfill a task. In communities, the I-Thou relationship predominates, whereas in institutions, the I-It relationship is at the forefront.

It is important that the Church, and more specifically our parishes, become loving, caring communities, where hospitality plays a central role, letting people know that they are important and welcome.

Changes in the Church and Society

Today, people desperately need to experience a sense of community that is often missing in their lives. Even though people may have an affluent lifestyle, they are searching for stability and meaning often in vain. No matter how much money people have, or their position in life, or how they conduct business, without God, a vacuum remains deep within. For this reason, people search for a community that cares about them and can help provide their lives with spiritual meaning.

A parish community that is hospitable, welcoming, and compassionate is more attractive than a parish that is merely administered efficiently.

When Mable, a domestic worker, suddenly died, her wake was held in the only meeting hall in the small village where she lived. Her relatives grieved her death terribly and needed care and understanding. They did not know the pastor of the Catholic Church in the village, so they were surprised when he showed up and gave a beautiful reflection. After it was over, a family member said, "If that's the kind of care and love that the Catholic Church is about, I'm going to find out more about this church."

Love and compassion attracted this family member to the church. The priest manifested what many Catholics often fail to sense in their parishes, namely welcome and hospitality. As a result, many do not claim membership in any parish nor regularly celebrate Sunday Mass. When dealing with them, they often say, "I don't practice any religion, because I get little out of formal church services. When I was a child, I prayed, learned about God, and my faith connected me to Jesus and the Church. As I matured and searched for compassionate answers in my church, I did not find them. Homilies were abstract reflections disconnected from my life. The liturgy did not speak to me, I felt little support, and the sex abuse scandal made me wary of believing what was said. Frankly, I lost trust."

Christianity is an interpersonal religion and spiritual nourishment requires connection with Jesus and his body, the Church. When teaching graduate and undergraduate theology classes at various Catholic universities, I often felt that God sent me to accompany the many students who did not connect with their parishes because they experienced indifference, meaningless homilies, or disagreements on matter of faith and morals.

We can connect alienated people like those students with a community that will help them fulfill their spiritual needs. We need to encourage them to find a Catholic faith community that supports them and can give vitality to their faith and meaning to their life.

It is a privilege to help searching Catholics find a parish where their soul can be nourished. Interpersonal contact in a caring parish makes all the difference for those searching to find meaning in a secular and changing society.

It is imperative for our faith community that young people identify with a parish that can also help them become a faith-filled family. In such a parish they will worship and receive support from the Christian community. This requires new efforts in parish evangelization, where families identify and respond favorably to hospitality, welcome, and compassion.

Changes in the Church and Society

FOR DISCUSSION

We now consider what effects the family, the people of God, and the faith community have in passing on the faith.

1. Discuss the influence that parents have on the faith formation of their children? What rituals might enhance a religious home environment.

2. How can a regular prayer life strengthen a child growing in today's secular wilderness?

3. Why is it important to commit the family to being a domestic church with all that this implies?

4. What does St. Paul's call to live a life of holiness mean for us today?

5. How would you suggest making your parish a vibrant, welcoming one?

6. What does the statement "Christianity is an interpersonal religion" mean for you and your parish?

7. Do you think that the Church has lost its attractive power today? Discuss.

5
ACTIVE LEADERSHIP

In our contemporary digital world, the Church needs a new style of leadership that will ensure a focus on the family and support active communities of faith. There is a need for compassionate pastoral leaders who ideally are also good administrators. This chapter considers credible leadership styles and the moral challenges that parish leaders face today.

LEADERSHIP STYLES

A vibrant parish requires a good leader. There are usually two types of leaders: transformational and transactional. A transformational leader motivates, inspires, and elevates a group to a higher purpose, often by interpersonal actions that encourage and support the members. A transactional leader gives priority to accomplishing the task at hand in a functional way. This includes organizing the group's efforts, making sure the budget is set, and carrying out the business and administrative matters that will make the organization successful in its goals.

Based on a meeting of priests in my diocese, it was revealed through a questionnaire that most pastors identified

Changes in the Church and Society

themselves primarily as transactional leaders while the associate pastors saw themselves as transformational leaders. A seasoned pastor stood up and said, "That's not fair! If you had asked the pastors when they were associate pastors the same question, they would have seen themselves as transformational leaders. Because of our administrative responsibilities, we have now become more transactional, for there is little time to do anything else."

His remarks indicated the challenge before clerical and lay pastoral leaders, or even parents, who spend much of their time doing functional work. They become overly immersed in administrative matters and often neglect people's ultimate needs.

This is a real challenge in today's environment, where parish reorganization requires pastors to lead three or more parishes, as they are given the task of consolidating multiple parish communities into one or two parishes. With this mandate, it is difficult for a priest or pastoral leader to be a transformational leader.

Parish reorganization is a major challenge for pastoral leaders who strive to maintain a transformational leadership style. They are often deluged with practical and administrative responsibilities in addition to the other duties of overseeing the smooth operation of a parish.

Furthermore, these challenges often distract pastors who are called to be ministers of care and compassion, qualities often not discernible if a pastor is deluged with functional administrative work. It is also difficult to increase vocations and respond to the various needs of parishioners if a pastor is viewed more as an administrator than as a shepherd of the flock.

Active Leadership

CREDIBILITY

Leadership is earned, not assigned. There was a time when most civic and church leaders were admired, and the person assuming a leadership position was trusted simply because he or she was the designated leader.

Today, because of credibility issues, those appointed as leaders need to prove themselves by being accepted by the group which the person is leading. This was exemplified recently by a new pastor who was appointed to a parish that had been led by a pastor for twenty years before he retired. The new pastor was never accepted by the congregation as their leader, largely because he insisted on things being done his way. He failed to listen to parishioners urging him to do otherwise.

It takes time for a leader to be accepted, trusted, and admired. Years ago, when a pastor was assigned for a long tenure, people were not so mobile. Consequently, leadership took on a different character. Now, pastors are appointed for shorter timeframes and people move often.

Today's parishioners are less likely to give pastors their loyalty until they get to know them. This is partly due to skepticism and some of the problems within the Church that we noted earlier. In addition, when a priest is assigned for a short tenure in a parish, he is less inclined to look to the long-term health of the parish and more likely to make short-term decisions regarding the parish ministry.

Regardless of how long a pastor serves a parish, he faces challenges to his leadership and credibility. Deeply rooted in a priest's lack of credibility is the mistrust generated by the sex abuse scandal and the response to this scandal by the bishops.

Changes in the Church and Society

Furthermore, this scandal has led many priests to shy away from significant ministry with younger people, thus widening the gap between the priest and his congregation. This has also had an impact on vocations that stemmed from sound, meaningful relationships between the priest and the youth of his parish.

There was a day when priests were implicitly trusted because they were priests. Today, they must win the trust of parishioners, which is a huge factor in building a vibrant parish community.

As the number of Catholics in the United States decreases and parishes close, the challenge to attract young people to the priesthood and religious life intensifies. When I was in high school, three laymen taught in our Catholic high school of eight hundred boys. The rest of our teachers were priests. Today, only laypeople teach there, with no full-time priests on the faculty. When I attended this school, about three graduates joined the seminary each year; now, the number is far fewer.

The closures and consolidation of parishes bring added burdens besides those already noted and challenge pastors to focus on their priorities. When a parish closes, it causes anger, frustration, and ambiguity. Such emotions exist in the parish where I ministered for thirty-eight years. When I first arrived, there was a pastor, an associate pastor, and myself. Following a parish reconfiguration, one pastor and two associate pastors minister to six different parishes and two schools. In such an arrangement, effective ministry is difficult. The pressures on the pastor to administer these parishes are immense and challenge his responsibility to attend to the spiritual needs of his flock.

Active Leadership

Most dioceses make efforts to help pastors deal with administrative issues, but support is also needed to minister to parishioners pastorally. In the aftermath of the 2019 pandemic and the declining church attendance, we ask: What do we want to pass on to future generations?

THE VIRTUE OF ACCOMPANIMENT

Today's parishes need faith leaders who are not only loyal to Church teaching and practice, but pastoral and compassionate in challenging situations.

In 1968, shortly after I joined the faculty at Mount St. Mary's Seminary in Cincinnati, numerous faculty discussions centered on whether Paul VI would change the Church's teaching on artificial birth control.

As we waited for the pope's decision, these discussions intensified. The faculty was split. Many believed that the pope would change the Church's teaching on artificial birth control, but a moral theology professor insisted that this pope would never change it. Finally, the pope issued his encyclical, *Humanae vitae*, reiterating the traditional stance of the Church not permitting artificial birth control.

The outcry following this encyclical was the first large-scale challenge to the Church's teaching authority during my life. Opposition to the pope's decision was widespread. Many married couples struggled with this issue, often making up their own minds.

Many theologians and Church historians note that this encyclical was the catalyst for the Church losing its role in shaping the Catholic conscience, as Catholics largely decided

Changes in the Church and Society

then for themselves on this and other matters. In addition, a major factor leading to the loss of Church credibility was rooted in the conflicts surrounding the ritual changes initiated by Vatican II. These included celebrating Mass in the vernacular, dropping mandatory Friday abstinence, changing the Lenten fast, and so on.

Changing such ritual patterns led the laity to question the authority of the Church and other Church teachings and set the stage for Catholics to disagree on matters like artificial birth control. Such disagreements also resulted in a loss of confidence regarding other moral questions including warfare, unmarried people living together, and issues surrounding homosexuality and same-sex marriage.

To address these divisions within the Church community, future pastoral leaders need to present the Church's teaching on disputed issues clearly and help Catholics form their own consciences on such matters. In so doing, it is of paramount importance that they show care and compassion in dealing with people struggling with moral issues and accompanying them on their journey to the truth.

Presenting Church teaching alone isn't sufficient, especially when a person is struggling with emotional and moral questions like gay marriage or birth control. Pastoral compassion is even more necessary. It is vital that those who struggle with such issues feel a sense of trust, acceptance, and compassion from pastoral ministers.

Supported by a pastoral attitude and a welcoming countenance by a church leader often helps a questioning person to thrive in their faith and form a correct conscience. A pastoral minister cannot change the Church's teaching but can make sure that a struggling person knows the Church's teaching and feels loved and trusted.

Above all, church leaders must be pastoral and practice the virtue of accompaniment. In complex human situations, taking time to help an inquirer form a correct conscience requires clarity about the Church's message and working with the person to develop the trust necessary in guiding a person through a challenging issue. At the same time, we need to be careful who we recommend when referring a person to someone for spiritual guidance. An overly rigorous pastoral minister can discourage an inquirer before a difficult conversation is initiated. A major goal in accompanying a person in their faith is to be sensitive to the person's situation while being true to Church teaching and showing compassion.

FOR DISCUSSION

We now consider how effective leadership effects passing on the faith.

1. Discuss transformational and transactional leadership in relation to various ministerial roles in your parish. How do they complement one another?

2. What do you see as the pastoral priorities of a pastor who is administering a large parish?

3. Can you think of examples when a pastoral minister has been trustworthy, accepting, and compassionate.

Changes in the Church and Society

4. What are the chief characteristics of effective leaders among young people?

5. If confronted with a difficult moral issue, with whom would you advise a friend to discuss the matter?

6. How would you describe the quality of leadership in your parish? What changes would you recommend?

7. In what ways can the Catholic Church improve the quality of its leaders? Discuss this regarding bishops, pastors, deacons, and pastoral ministers.

6

POPE FRANCIS AND PASTORAL LEADERSHIP

When stressing the importance of pastoral leadership and compassionate listening, it helps to remember Pope Francis's focus on accompaniment and walking with families in their joys and sorrows. In this regard, chapter 8 of *Amoris laetitia*, his post-synodal apostolic exhortation addressing the pastoral care of families, discusses controversial issues, including gay marriage and the reception of Holy Communion by divorced persons who have not received a declaration of nullity.

Pope Francis says that "the Church must accompany with attention and care the weakest of her children, who show signs of a wounded and troubled love, by restoring in them hope and confidence, like the beacon of a light house in a port or a torch carried among the people to enlighten those who have lost their way or who are in the midst of a storm" (*Relatio Synodi* 2014, 28).

Changes in the Church and Society

To address Pope Francis's pastoral focus, this chapter discusses this "new way of seeing" and the notion of accompaniment.

A NEW WAY OF SEEING

While remaining faithful to basic Catholic beliefs and practices, *Amoris laetitia* calls for a new way of looking at pastoral issues, not unlike the approach taken at the Second Vatican Council. Pope Francis offers us this new way of seeing and ministering by using expressions like "dialogue," "accompaniment," "communication," and "encounter."

In so doing, he urges us to take people where they are and walk with them on their faith journey. He invites us to embrace a new way of thinking, counseling, reconciling penitents, preaching, and teaching. In theological terms, this often means shifting our perspective from an abstract, deductive, rule-oriented approach to a more historical, inductive, and conscience-centered one.

Pope Francis stresses the importance of dialogue, accompaniment, and engagement. He focuses on the concrete, the here-and-now situation in which people find themselves, and on conscience. His approach does not question how the Church mediates the Holy Spirit's presence through her teaching, norms, liturgical practices, and rules. While maintaining the vital role of the Church, Pope Francis implies that God often deals directly with us in our joys and sorrows and focuses on the complex realities that we face.

He reaffirms that our loving God is present in our difficult situations, guiding us in ways that go beyond human comprehension. In this context, Pope Francis urges priests, counselors, and Christian disciples to address the issue of conscience, accompany those in need, and help them discern the designs of God.

Pope Francis further articulates the direction taken at Vatican II and in the papacies of Saint John Paul II and Pope Benedict XVI. He refocuses some trends in ecclesiology, moral theology, and pastoral practice while maintaining a basic continuity with traditional Church teachings and practices.

Concerning more controversial issues, Pope Francis invites us to probe more deeply into the role of conscience, while not minimizing the significance of the Church's norms of moral conduct. He also challenges us to take a deeper look at pastoral ministry, in other words, accompanying people in their joys and sorrows, especially when they need us most. It means sacrificing ourselves in traumatic moments of sickness and death and having the courage to fall on our knees and wash the feet of broken people before us, as the woman wiped Jesus's feet, and as Jesus washed the feet of his disciples at the Last Supper.

It is by accompanying families in their joys and sorrows that pastoral leaders receive new vigor. To assist in this, though, the education commission, pastoral council, liturgical committee, and finance council of the parish must be oriented toward the family. In so doing, the parish gains a "family perspective," that the United Stated Bishops recommended at the end of the last millennium.

Parish leaders need to be reminded that the most powerful influence on families is the secular culture that engulfs them. By embracing a family perspective, the parish must consider

Changes in the Church and Society

the cultural situation of people in their everyday work, play, and lifestyle.

With this renewed perspective, pastoral leaders focus on the evangelization that happens within the family. It highlights the family's commitment to their faith and catechetical learning. Consequently, parish leaders benefit by seeing parish evangelization in light of early Christian house churches, where family members learned that a vital part of a Christian home was its missionary outreach beyond the family. In so doing, family members who accept their responsibility to share the good news in the home are motivated to participate in parish ministry and share the message of Jesus and his mission with the world.

Finally, to make this viable, pastoral leaders must have a hope-filled, positive attitude in the spirit of Pope Francis as they dialogue with people and accompany them on their journey.

ACCOMPANIMENT

A personal event that occurred in spring 2016 had a profound effect on my attitude toward ministry and the significant role of accompaniment.

My sister, Joan, and I, were filled with uncertainty as we drove to Columbus, Ohio, to visit our dying brother, Tom, at the James Cancer Hospital. On the journey to see Tom for the last time, we remembered our other sister, Mary Ann, seriously ill in Cincinnati at Good Samarian Hospital.

After arriving, we waited outside his room. When he saw us, he invited us to enter, where we gathered with family and friends. Once everyone else had left the room, Joan and

I remained with him. I asked Tom, "Do you want us to pray with you?" He answered, "Sure!" As we recited the Our Father, I looked at his trembling lips and Joan's concerned expression.

When we reached words, "Thy kingdom come," my mind remembered my mother teaching us this prayer when we were young and praying it together with Mary Ann, Joan, Tom, and me. It was almost as if we had been transported back to our childhood to experience a core moment that united us and had brought us to faith.

I had never experienced what Pope Francis calls "accompaniment" more powerfully than at this wounded, vulnerable moment and as we prayed, "Give us this day our daily bread." Throughout our lives, I remembered how our family nourished each other in faith, joy, and sorrow, made possible by faith-filled parents.

That day, as I left Tom's room, not long before he died, I realized more deeply that faith is born in and nourished by the family—where we grow in love, mercy, and forgiveness through life's concrete events.

This story, hopefully, invites us to reflect on the influence that we have on others and they on us. It especially invites us to reach out to the wounded and hurting, as we thank God for the blessings we have received.

In so doing, we recall St. Paul's final words to the Thessalonians: "May the God of peace himself sanctify you entirely; and may your spirit and soul and body be kept sound and blameless at the coming of our Lord Jesus Christ. The one who calls you is faithful, and he will do this. Beloved, pray for us" (1 Thess 5:23–25).

Changes in the Church and Society

FOR DISCUSSION

We now consider how pastoral sensitivity challenges passing on the faith.

1. How can the Church help its members better appreciate that the most powerful influence on families is the secular culture that engulfs them?

2. How can parents help their children appreciate the sacredness of all life?

3. Why does Pope Francis stress the importance of dialogue, accompaniment, and engagement.

4. As our society becomes more secularized and atheism grows, why is it especially important for the Church to adopt more of a family perspective?

5. Why do you think a positive, pastoral attitude in the spirit of Pope Francis is important for pastoral leaders, and what practical ways can this be lived out in your parish?

6. What does it mean to uphold the dignity of every person, regardless of their age or background?

7. In what ways can you accompany people in your family and parish community? Why do you think this approach to evangelization is important?

7
A MISSION-FOCUSED CHURCH

With Pope Francis's pastoral perspective on accompaniment in mind, let us now address directions that need to be taken toward a mission-focused church. These directions include a church that is humble, the church's mission to youth, the challenge of clericalism, and meeting people's needs.

A HUMBLE CHURCH

Since we follow Jesus as our leader, Pope Francis encourages the Church to give humble witness to the world. His humble example as pope encourages Church members and leaders to do the same. This humility is manifested in the living quarters that the pope chose, following his election as pope, his regular visits to the poor in Rome, and his genuine concern for migrants and refugees.

Changes in the Church and Society

A major challenge facing the Church's missionary endeavors will be to address how the Church attracts young people and inactive Catholics to become active members. Their continued defection from the faith is a strong indicator that something must be done to shift the culture of the Catholic community. A clue for encouraging young people to get involved in the Church and become missionary disciples is their desire to work with the poor and disenfranchised in the spirit of Pope Francis.

Such a ministry reflects how the Church images Christ to the world. In so doing, Christians become authentic followers of the humble man from Nazareth who attracted followers. Theology, advertising, or a return to traditional liturgical practices will not accomplish this goal.

Attracting new members and keeping those currently practicing the faith must be rooted in Jesus's call to welcome. This call to live the Christian faith in a way that inspires and attracts others to follow Jesus demands humility. It acknowledges that the Church does not have all the answers but is open to learning, especially in her outreach to the poor and needy. Accompanying this call to minister to the poor, the Church must pray and worship together to inspire others.

For the Church to be missionary today, it is important to ask, "What type of parish community are we preparing for our children and young adults?" Youth are searching for something different from what Catholics sought in days past. Increasingly, though, parish membership consists of elderly people, with fewer young members. Parishes need to focus their missionary endeavors on the future generations of Catholics.

What, then, do young people look for in a parish? They look for authenticity, support, and a place where like-minded believers energize one another. They hope for a supportive community of believers and a message that makes sense. They look for knowledgeable leaders, humble enough to admit they do not know all the answers but willing to accompany them in the search for God's will on their journey.

In addition, Catholics need a deeper understanding of the Mass and sacraments. They look for a place where they hear God's word that offers a path forward when addressing civic, moral, and ethical issues. Difficult challenges can only be addressed in a humble Church that searches for ways to convince people that the Holy Spirit is leading them to follow the path that Jesus walked centuries ago.

MISSION TO YOUNG PEOPLE

The Church is especially concerned about its mission to young people. The number of young people leaving the church is a serious matter, one that requires special attention. What will the Church be like if many young people leave before adulthood?

Often, the young people, who are not active members of the parish, attended Catholic schools, but their Catholicism does not reach further than the school door. This does not mean they are not good people. Most are wonderful young members of society, but for them, practicing the faith into which they were initiated at baptism is not a priority.

We don't need data from polling agencies to know this information. We can simply observe what's happening in our parishes on Sundays, where a low percentage of Catholic teenagers are present. This is reason enough to investigate

Changes in the Church and Society

this situation for unless the root cause of this decrease in active membership is addressed, the decline will continue.

The issue of leaving the Church does not apply to all young Catholics, for many are loyal to their faith, work with the poor, and perform other ministerial activities. Yet, active involvement today in the Church includes too small a percentage of youth.

With growing uncertainty about the future, an increase in violence in society, economic and job insecurity, and the impact these factors have on society in general, our young people need guidance more than ever. Such guidance can come from the Church, if church leaders work together to help them connect with their parishes and other church organizations that can provide positive guidance and direction.

Of course, such an initiative to support our young people must start with their bishops and pastors. Admittedly, such support is no easy task, considering the influence of secularism on Catholic young people and adults. Nevertheless, the youth are the future missionaries of the Church, and we must prepare them for their mission.

THE CHALLENGE OF CLERICALISM

The ecclesial attempts to address the challenges to the Church's mission and ministry reflect a growing tendency toward a more traditional Church. This trend exists in seminaries, priestly circles, among some of the laity, and even in the bishops' conference.

Unfortunately, the mission and ministry of the Church present across various dioceses reveal a divided Church and

A Mission-Focused Church

points to fundamental differences in church leadership that have repeatedly been addressed by Pope Francis. He indicates that the clash between the traditional and more progressive members of the Church is a real challenge to its vitality and growth.

In any organization, when there are uncertainties in a changing paradigm, it is not good to return to the old way of doing things. Once the new paradigm has been unleashed—as it was at Vatican II and beyond—the genie cannot be put back in the bottle, as if it is business as usual.

Now, many adults and young people who actively participate in the Church and attend Sunday Mass grew up in traditional Catholic families. This trend affects the direction that the Church's missionary outreach to families takes in parishes throughout the world.

The style of some church leaders today is manifested in the reemergence of a more traditional form of priestly formation. In fact, many men enter the seminary with the desire to be formed in this more traditional way. Consequently, after ordination, their ecclesiology and liturgical practices are also more traditional. This trend continues throughout their priesthood so that there is now a division between some younger priests and more progressive older priests. This is reflected by the latter wearing informal garb and the former often appearing in more clerical attire.

In addition, differences exist between the bishops who follow the style of Pope Francis and those who seek a more traditional style. The differences between these two polarities in the Church is an internal issue that must be faced, as Pope Francis recently emphasized in a meeting with priests at the Vatican.

Changes in the Church and Society

Today, as the gulf in some Church circles between clergy and laity widens, clericalism increases. Unless addressed openly, this leads to growing tensions and a less open Church. It is paradoxical that at the precise time that Pope Francis calls for a less clerical, more open synodal Church, the opposite is emerging. Where this tension takes us is not clear, but it will affect the missionary role of the Church. The Church cannot return to a closed Church of the past, for our contemporary society demands new.

MEETING PEOPLE'S NEEDS

Effective missionary leaders place a high priority on the needs of their peoples. This priority necessarily includes investigating deeper the reasons there is a decline in Catholicism. Is the Church connecting spiritually with her members? In this regard, there is a need for spiritual renewal of the laity, based on faith, one rooted in love and justice, following the dictates of the gospel.

Effective pastoring requires a faith that is rooted in the home, reinforced in the parish, and supported by like-minded Christians. The clergy and laity need to develop parish communities of faith where people of all ages can be renewed and fulfill their needs for justice, love, and meaning.

Meeting people's needs is the first step to active participation in a parish. We learn this from research data, but even more from listening to the voices of the laity in parishes, where they feel at home and welcome.

We live in a new world, and the future Church demands new modes of presence and interpersonal communication.

A Mission-Focused Church

This Church in the United States will be smaller; whether it will be more dynamic remains to be seen.

Today, many people search for a faith tradition that will satisfy their spiritual needs—providing spiritual advice on how to live more meaningful lives than the secular world offers. They search for meaning in a troubled world, and the Catholic Church must address their pressing needs and provide a welcoming community of like-minded believers to counter the elements of secularism that lead them away from God. Consequently, the Church of tomorrow must ascertain the needs of its member and develop pastoral styles that meet those needs. This includes liturgical celebrations that bring the Father, Son, and Holy Spirit into the lives of their members and build faith-filled families.

Initially, the changes at Vatican II were difficult to accept, but gradually, most Catholics saw their benefits and blessings and gave them new insights into developing a more mature faith, not guided primarily by rules and obligations, but by the Holy Spirit working within them. On reflection, most older Catholics would probably not want to return to a pre–Vatican II Church.

Many younger Catholics never knew the beauty and rigor of this pre–Vatican II Church but may have heard about the clarity and certitude of its teaching. This clarity and certitude may attract many young people today who struggle with the uncertainty of society in general and conclude that what is needed now is a stable foundation that seemed to be present in the Church prior to Vatican II. They emphasize devotions and eucharistic adoration to complement their sacramental life. While the view that a traditional approach may afford stability, it often fails to appreciate and even accept the many positive achievements and advances of Vatican II.

In the first part of this book, we noted that when paradigm shifts occur, and later modifications are desired, it does not help to go backward to regain the shining moment initially unleashed by the new paradigm. Rather, we must begin anew from where we are now in striving to find where God is leading us today.

In this process, it is necessary to maintain the essentials of faith and not confuse our spirituality with incidental aspects of its practice, that is, avoiding rubrics and actions that are not connected with the here and now.

If an imbalance occurred in the post–Vatican II Church, the same can be said of the current trend to a traditional Church with its insistence on certain beliefs and practices, like requiring all parishioners receive Holy Communion on the tongue. This is not the answer. Such subjective decisions on the part of some pastoral leaders can drive people away from the Church and is often out of touch with people's real needs.

The different trends within the Church concern Pope Francis, who urges better communication between the extremes and those in between on matters like Church governance, synodality, liturgical practices, and basic beliefs. It is important for this generation to pass on a reconciled rather than a fractured Church that will guide us into the future.

FOR DISCUSSION

We now consider how a mission-focused Church influences passing on the faith.

A Mission-Focused Church

1. Jesus sent his disciples into the world to convert it. Why is the notion of a mission- focused Church important today?

2. What does it mean to be a humble Church. In our secular world, why is humility especially significant today?

3. What are some of the primary factors influencing the effectiveness of the Church's approach to young people today? What significant efforts do you recommend to attract young people to the Church today?

4. There is a strong traditional movement in the Church today that is reminiscent of pre–Vatican II. What are the pros and cons of this movement?

5. What are the reasons for this traditional movement in the Church today?

6. What are the positive and negative influences that technological advances can have on the Church's missionary role today?

7. What recommendations would you offer your bishop to strengthen the missionary outreach in your parish or diocese?

Part III
The Future of Catholicism

~~~~~~

Although the Church has a long history, it remains ever new through the energizing power of the Holy Spirit who continually brings her new life. With confidence in the Holy Spirit's abiding presence, the Church moves forward with hope, as she faces the challenges beset her from the wider culture and within the Church that were outlined in the first two parts of this book.

To move forward with hope requires a commitment to Jesus's abiding presence, a faith-filled community of believers, committed Christian families, solid leadership, collaboration throughout the Catholic community, and an openness to discerning where the Holy Spirit is leading the Church. Hope is the motivator for renewal and the dynamic that leads Catholics to believe and act.

The Changing Face of Catholicism

To revitalize communal and ministerial efforts, the dream of Solomon at Gibeon offers us the way on our hope-filled journey (cf. 1 Kgs 3:4–15). In this passage, God appeared to Solomon in a dream, not long after he became king of the Israelites. Solomon said he was inexperienced and just a child. God asked him, "Ask what I should give you?" (1 Kgs 3:5b). Solomon did not ask for gold, power, or pleasure, but an understanding mind and heart. In other words, Solomon asked God for wisdom.

Like the inexperienced Solomon, the Church today needs to ask God for wisdom in coping with the challenges of the secular world and those within the Church. As with Solomon in his time, hope is essential for the future of the Church.

In outlining new directions for a hope-filled Church, this third part focuses on hope as it addresses new ethnic populations, the law of love, and the Church's relevance. It imagines a new awakening of faith in light of Jesus's missionary mandate and evangelization. Finally, it brings God's message of hope into focus by emphasizing the importance of the family in the Church's renewed efforts to create vibrant communities of faith.

8
LOOKING AHEAD

As the Church moves forward, major challenges must be faced, and opportunities embraced to fulfill her mission and ministry. The challenges and opportunities that we will consider in this chapter include reaching out to new ethnic populations, striving for justice and charity, and addressing the relevance of the Church in the world today.

NEW ETHNIC POPULATIONS

Endless possibilities for Church renewal exist in the talents and faith of Hispanic, Asian, and other ethnic denominations throughout the country. Catholicism in the United States has a history of being renewed by newcomers to our shores. In the nineteenth century, immigrants from Ireland, Germany, Italy, and other European countries changed the face of Catholicism. Largely because of troubles in their homelands, people arrived here and became the backbone of the Catholic faith in America.

Soon after my grandmother arrived in Cincinnati from Holland, she and her parents moved from downtown to the Price Hill suburbs. As a girl of eleven, she was profoundly

The Future of Catholicism

moved by her parish church there. She often told us that when she first saw St. Lawrence Church, she just stood and gazed at its magnificence. It became her parish for the rest of her life. The church, which is still standing, connected her with her Catholic roots in Holland.

Whenever I attend Mass in this architectural wonder, I imagine my grandma sitting in the same spot. She and her subsequent family were married and celebrated their Catholic faith here. In her bedroom, grandma kept a painting of the Sacred Heart and other religious images—lifelong reminders that the faith she first professed in Europe was still alive in her new home in America.

I now have this painting and her other sacred images in my home. When looking at them, I recall another painting of the Holy Family in my sitting room at St. Clare Church, a gift given to me by an Asian family who recently emigrated from the Philippines to Cincinnati. They too, brought their devotional life from Asia and profess it in this country.

This painting of the Holy Family reminds me that, just as my grandmother's family and others like hers strengthened the Catholic faith here in America in the 1800s, so are immigrants from around the globe strengthening it today.

Today, immigrants come mostly from Asia or from Hispanic-speaking countries in central and south America. Many are from troubled countries and set a new tone for the future of Catholicism in the United States.

Spanish is now required in seminary formation programs, and Hispanic and Asian bishops have been appointed to the U.S. hierarchy. In addition, the Church has taken on social justice initiatives and supported immigrants, especially those

Looking Ahead

coming through our southern border, and will gradually assimilate many of them into Catholic parishes.

When nineteenth-century immigrants arrived, they maintained their faith by joining existing parishes or establishing new ones that supported their Catholic identity. Immigrant groups continue to join existing parishes but maintaining their Catholic identity has become more challenging.

They are especially vulnerable to the influence of a powerful secular environment, imbued into them by easy access to the Internet, cell phones, and television. In addition, other Christian groups invite them to join their congregations. This is particularly true in large evangelical and smaller storefront churches.

The future vitality of Catholicism will be strongly influenced by the support parishes extend to new immigrants. As Cardinal Bernardin of Chicago said at the Los Angeles Religious Education Congress at the beginning of the new millennium, "We must face the issue of evangelizing the new immigrants. If we fail to adequately address their spiritual needs, many will leave us. The struggle to maintain them in the Church is going on today. We cannot neglect them."

The enormous challenge of addressing the spiritual needs of immigrants to the United States can be seen across the country. An example of this was evident at a flea market in a Cincinnati mall.

As I walked through this large flea market situated in a mercantile building, everything seemed to be on sale. Customers were attracted by bargains but also by the hospitality and welcome of the various owners selling inside the mall. As I meandered through the shops and booths, I noticed that a section of the mall was a meeting place for Spanish-speaking

The Future of Catholicism

people. They gathered there every weekend for mutual support and to purchase items from their native countries.

It was in a particularly attractive part of the mall, one with a strong Hispanic flavor, and a great place to evangelize and support immigrants from Mexico and South America.

The area included a large section set aside for a Protestant evangelical church booth, established to evangelize the Hispanics who did not feel welcome in mainline Catholic parishes, which had made no special provisions for Spanish-speaking Catholics.

The scene reminded me of what it may have been like for the early disciples going into the marketplace to proclaim God's Word. With them in mind, I also pictured recent immigrants who gravitated toward this spiritual enclave within the flea market to find God, arrange for a marriage or the baptism of their child in this evangelical church.

The Catholic Church belongs here, providing booths in this and similar malls to answer people's questions and invite Hispanic immigrants to local Catholic parishes. Most of the people shopping here had been baptized as Catholics before immigrating to the United States.

With the uncertainty in today's Catholic parishes, especially the priest shortage and the realization that the Catholic population is declining, Catholic parishioners need to reach out and invite immigrant Catholics to their local parishes.

Having a Catholic booth in a flea market is a small but symbolic step, inviting us to do more for immigrants. Our missionary calling includes passing on the faith to others, as previous generations of Americans passed it on to our ancestors.

Looking Ahead

THE LAW OF LOVE

As with any ministry, love of God and neighbor is the foundation of all missionary endeavors. This love, expressed early in our life through our family, complements the basic goodness existing in every person. The law of love, taught by Jesus, is the fundamental norm required for living virtuous lives and influencing others to follow Christ. When people strive to live by love of God and neighbor, expressed in a family and witnessed in a parish community, they are on their way to recognizing the role of faith in every aspect of their lives.

Fostering a virtuous life is not easy. As children grow, they need role models who can demonstrate the positive values learned early in a family that lead to moral righteousness. When parents teach their children the meaning of love through their good example, they establish a path for them to follow.

I still recall the influence that the good example of my father had on me as a child. One event of special significance happened every year during Holy Week, and usually on Good Friday. Even though we were very busy in our dry goods store just before Easter, as we needed the income from our sales to support our family, my dad would tell us to help the customers as best we could until he returned. Then, he went to St. Augustine's Church for prayer and confession so that he could make the best possible Easter. I still remember him putting on his hat and watching him walk up the street, only to return about forty-five minutes later. This simple act of devotedness had profound meaning for me throughout the rest of my life.

If, however, a parent cuts corners and resorts to immoral or unjust activities, they negatively influence the moral compass that a child develops. What children learn at home is also strongly influenced by their peers. In the predigital era, such influence was largely limited to the example of boys or girls living in the same home or neighborhood. Today, the gamut of influence for right or wrong includes peers they meet online.

Many obstacles stand in the way of developing attitudes that are consistent with solid religious values. We are influenced by the cultural norms assimilated from technology and social media. In this context, the parish can play an important role in teaching and celebrating the love of God, manifested most fully in the love of Jesus.

Although society generally strives toward what is just, injustice and dishonesty can be found everywhere. It is imperative that parents and teachers exercise just practices at home, in school, and in the community, for just living is at the heart of being Catholic.

The Church has a rich history of social justice practices. It is a powerful reminder of the importance of living justly that provides an anchor for a good moral life. Such practices begin in one's family and extend to friends and neighbors. When we realize that all humans are created equal and have the same rights, it becomes clearer which actions are just and moral, and why we need the moral support of the Church.

Jesus commissioned the Church to preach the message of justice to the whole world. Among other things, this commission includes exercising justice toward employees by paying them just salaries, while encouraging others to do the same. It challenges Catholic organizations to change any of their own practices if they are unjust. To counter unjust behavior, communication and transparency are essential.

Looking Ahead

RELEVANCE OF THE CHURCH

From early Christianity through the Middle Ages, the Church was the patroness of the arts and sciences. In most instances, the Christian worldview influenced the tenor and direction of artistic works and scientific discoveries.

As secularism gained influence throughout humanity, the Church began to exercise less influence on the thought and direction of scientific and artistic work. Increasingly, we find differences between the moral teachings and practices of science and technology, on the one hand, and Church teachings and practice, on the other.

The trend toward materialism influences our educational system. Catholic grade and high schools decline in numbers, and some Catholic universities become more secularized. The Church no longer subsidizes the research and direction of what is required in a post-religious world.

The result is a growing dichotomy between the values put forward by a secular society and the religious values of Catholicism. For all intents and purposes, it means that the Church needs to focus its message on values that are vital aspects of Jesus's teachings. These must be inculcated into our secular society in this twenty-first century.

This focus means connecting Christian values with the digital paradigm, so prevalent in our lives. In this context, the Word of God must address the needs of people who seek wisdom, clarity, and spiritual formation. It also means that the Church needs strong, dynamic, and faith-filled spiritual leaders and a committed laity who love the Church and strive to evangelize the world. Without credibility and commitment,

Christian values will have little influence in a secular materialistic culture.

Because of the sexual abuse scandal and the other issues that we have mentioned, the Church needs to focus on matters of faith if it is to regain credibility. These matters of faith include the Eucharist, evangelization, and social justice. It is worthwhile reflecting on how the early Church converted the pagan Roman Empire often through teaching Jesus's law of love. Of course, such a focus requires a commitment to the domestic church. It is primarily in the home that Catholicism can be revitalized, along with the support of parishes to assist parents in their role of salvation.

When future generations recognize the special gifts that a believing Church has to offer, society can begin to find what is essential for true happiness. In short, the Church must renew her commitment to bring Jesus's message of love to the secular society.

Consequently, for the Church to become relevant in today's world, we must probe deeper into the values that lead to inner happiness rather than adopt the superficial happiness of the secular world. By being grounded in her Christian past, the Church can reveal new avenues of faith and offer this gift of faith to future generations.

FOR DISCUSSION

We now consider what is needed to pass on the faith.

1. How can the Church impact society and move people to see the importance of the Catholic faith? What roles do you think technology and personal presence have in this effort?

Looking Ahead

2. How can your parish become more sensitive to the needs of its parishioners?

3. How can your parish reach out to migrants and other ethnic populations coming into your neighborhood or city?

4. In what ways did the Catholic Church impact you, your family, or friends when your ancestors first arrived in this country? What does this impact tell you about the future Church?

5. How can your parish increase its ministry of social justice?

6. What do you think is the most important influence on a young person's commitment to their faith?

7. Do you think that Catholicism is becoming irrelevant for young people? If so, what can you and your parish do to enhance its significance for the next generation?

9

A NEW AWAKENING OF FAITH

There are three aspects of our faith that should give us hope regarding the future of the Church. The first is the words of Jesus, who promised that the gates of hell will not prevail against his Church (cf. Matt 16:18). These words console us knowing that the Spirit is leading the Church and will remain with us, regardless of the circumstances until the end of time.

The second aspect that should give us hope is the basic truths of the Church that get handed down from generation to generation. Even in trying times, the Church must remain faithful to Christ and his message.

The third aspect that gives us hope and allows the faith to grow is the unity of the Church centered around the leadership and guidance of the pope and bishops and the missionary response of Christians to fulfill Jesus's injunction to teach all nations that flows from this unity.

So far, we have considered the challenges that influence the future of Catholicism. Now, we consider those elements that give us hope and help us to maintain a vibrant faith for future generations.

A New Awakening of Faith

The evangelizing mandate of the Church includes the following dimensions:

- The evangelical nature of the Church is missionary. Jesus commissioned us to teach all nations, which is a motivating factor for a vibrant community. This evangelical mission begins with the family.
- The evangelical ministry consists of the ministries of word, worship, and service.
- The Church's evangelical efforts are fulfilled by the family, the parish, and Christian service in the marketplace.

The evangelical mandate of Jesus is the framework for passing on faith to those who come after us when proclaiming the word of God, celebrating it through the sacraments, and especially the Mass, and serving the people of God. These ministries connect Jesus's call to evangelize with the thoughts, feelings, and needs of God's people.

JESUS'S MISSIONARY MANDATE

In the early years of my priesthood, I learned that a missionary disciple is called to work alongside a pastor in a parish. Prior to this, I had never connected being a missionary for Jesus with the parish community. I believed that missionaries were only sent to rural areas or foreign countries to spread the word of God.

Even though I do not use the word *mission* for the events that I describe below, my experience points to a deeper realization of what it means to be a missionary disciple of Christ. It is this realization that helped me to appreciate the importance for a missionary to connect Jesus and his message with people's minds and hearts. In other words, a missionary strives to connect to the "within" of people, thereby moving them to external action, like following Christ's call for social justice. How did Jesus do this? Perhaps a story will help.

Early in my priesthood, my pastor gave me list of seven people and asked me to contact them. He said they might be interested in finding out about the Church. I followed up upon his request and asked four other parishioners to join me. The following three episodes sum up what I learned from the visits made to the people on the pastor's list about the significance of touching the "within" of these individuals and so move them externally, from "without," to consider becoming Catholic.

The first episode involved meeting with an elderly and lonely man. He was open to anything that filled the void for meaning and God in his heart. Reaching out to him in kindness and getting him involved in parish functions revitalized him and prepared him to enter the Church with joy and hope.

The second episode concerned a middle-aged, divorced woman and her teenage daughter, and the impact and influence we can be to others. For this meeting, I asked a married couple to accompany me. At first, the woman declined our visit, but then her daughter told her that she was a friend of the daughter of the married couple. After learning of this connection, the divorced woman's attitude changed, and they welcomed our visits. Both the mother and daughter were Catholic but were not going to church. After several visits, the daughter convinced her mom to return to Church.

A New Awakening of Faith

The third episode involved visits to an elderly couple's home, where I was welcomed with enthusiasm. The wife was Catholic; the husband was not. On one occasion, I commented that I noticed that they both attended Mass together every Sunday. I then asked the husband, "Have you ever thought about becoming a Catholic?" With tears in his eyes, he answered, "I've been waiting twenty years for someone to ask me that question." He entered the Church at the Easter vigil that same year.

In each episode, those who accepted Jesus were inspired by someone striking a chord within them. In other words, our kindness, care, and compassion touched their hearts and allowed them to respond to the grace of God.

Evangelization is not complex; it happens in the simplest ways, when a parent, neighbor, or church leader speaks to people's hearts, and enables the person to change.

Later, when I told these stories to Marie, a young mother, she spoke of her infant son and said, "While looking at Joshua, I wonder how I can best pass on the faith to him." Her words remind us of Christians through the ages, who accepted Jesus's missionary mandate to pass on the faith to their children as an essential aspect of following him.

Many Christians have sacrificed their lives in testimony to their beliefs. Willing to do so, they accepted their responsibility to spread their faith in Jesus Christ. They regarded the missionary mandate as paramount in their lives. They not only believed this for themselves but embraced their call to share Jesus's message with their family and friends.

When reflecting on what we hope to pass on to those who come after us, Marie's words remind us of the primary importance of our faith.

The Future of Catholicism

EVANGELIZATION

Evangelization has been an ongoing process within the Christian community since the early Church. It seeks to initiate people ever more deeply into the mystery of God's love, revealed most fully in the dying and rising of Jesus.

Evangelization involves an intentional action, a conscious realization that Jesus calls us to share in the "good news" through word and action. The process of evangelization seeks to unlock the mystery of God's love, revealed in Jesus.

Catholic evangelization is a communal affair. Jesus, the "good news," comes to us through the Christian community. Although many individuals evangelize, when fulfilling Jesus's missionary mandate, evangelization is never only a "me-and-Jesus" event. It is an action of the entire Christian community under the guidance of the Holy Spirit.

Whether the Church's missionary activities are manifested through a parish, a domestic Church, or an individual, the faith is passed on in the name of the Church.

All Church ministries are aspects or moments in the evangelization process. In a family, evangelization begins with the love of parents and continues as they teach their children to grow in faith. Prayer is nurtured in their home, which is a domestic church.

Catholic schools are a vital extension of the domestic church. Here, children grow in the faith that is influenced by the Catholic environment of the school through prayer, catechesis, liturgy, and service ministries that present opportunities for evangelization.

The opportunity for individual Catholics to evangelize can occur in various ways. For example, when a store clerk shows kindness and respect to customers, or a high school student is truthful, they implicitly evangelize by their good example.

There is nothing new about evangelization. Catholics have always evangelized, even though we may not have always used this word to describe the process. As a child, my parents laid the foundation of evangelization through their good example, prayer, and the simple ways they catechized us about Jesus, the Church, and the communion of saints.

Of course, participating in the rich sacramental life of the Church has always been an important aspect of evangelization. When we pray our morning offering to God, our whole day becomes an act of evangelization that gives glory to God. These acts of evangelization create an environment that sets the tone for what happens in the home, where a Christian family lives and loves.

Evangelization has three components: the ministry of the word, the ministry of worship, and the ministry of service. These three components can be viewed as three strong branches, coming from the trunk of an evangelization tree, rooted in the rich soil of the paschal mystery. Let's now reflect on each of these components and how faith is passed down from generation to generation.

Ministry of the Word

Every religion is rooted in fundamental beliefs. These beliefs are often based on a creation story centered around gods or a God. In the Judeo-Christian tradition, the creation stories in Genesis centers on the one God and origin of all life (cf. Gen 1—2).

In the early Church, beginning with apostles and the first followers of Jesus, the faith community accepted its responsibility by passing on the basic teachings of Christianity that centered on the paschal mystery—the life, death, and resurrection of Jesus.

Knowledge of the basic teachings of faith is essential and highlights the importance of passing on our faith to our children through a strongly faith-filled home environment. By intentionally creating a spiritual environment in their family, parents teach their children the fundamentals of faith, as they grow and mature.

After Vatican II, the Church put increased emphasis on teaching the fundamentals of faith from womb to tomb. This was called "total religious education" and included adult faith formation, but in recent years, quality catechesis and the priority given to it has declined.

This is evident in parishes and dioceses where significant reductions have occurred in staffing and funds allocated for catechetical ministry. Dioceses and parishes must remember that catechesis is an important aspect of evangelization.

An essential aspect of evangelization or passing on the faith includes making sure that families, parishes, and Catholic schools, maintain a vibrant catechesis. In simplest form this means:

- making sure that the fundamentals of faith are presented. These include the belief in God, that Jesus is Lord, and that the Church is the Body of Christ, and so on; and
- catechizing in such a way that those being instructed understand what is taught.

The method used to catechize is a means to an end. For catechesis to be effective, the method must connect with

A New Awakening of Faith

those being catechized and the basic beliefs of the faith must be understood and practiced. Faith cannot be passed on if children and adults are not properly instructed.

Ministry of Worship

The ministry of worship, or celebrating liturgy, is the second component of evangelization. When considering the future of Catholicism and what we hope to pass on to future generations, we must consider liturgy, especially the Mass.

The question of declining Mass attendance often arises whenever priests and laity discuss the future of the Church. As noted earlier, Catholics of all ages are falling away from the Church and fewer young people attend Mass on Sundays. This occurs even though they go to Catholic high schools.

To respond to this concern, the following questions are important:

- *Have we adequately catechized young people to know and appreciate the Mass and the other sacraments?* It used to be the case that when young people, who had stopped going to church, became adults and got married, they would often return to the Church. This is not as common now. The impact of secular society is so strong that many do not recognize the value of their Catholic faith in their lives.
- *Do we encourage our youth to make an intentional commitment to the faith, recognizing that there is a God, that Jesus is Lord, and the Church is the Body of Christ?* This means helping them to internalize their spirituality and fulfill their

moral responsibilities. Furthermore, we need to encourage our youth to realize that the Eucharist is the ongoing celebration of the dying and rising of Christ. In other words, he comes to us in the Eucharist under the appearance of bread and wine, and we are enabled to go forth as his disciples.
- *Do parents recognize that they are the greatest positive influence in passing on the faith to their children?* Youth catechesis becomes far more challenging if parents no longer attend Mass regularly on Sundays, or they are not nurturing the faith by creating a domestic church within the home.

In responding to these questions, parishes must take the necessary steps to pass on the faith through vibrant liturgies, including the Mass and other sacramental actions that are tangible expressions of our relationship with God and our Lord.

God's divine plan is revealed in all the sacraments but especially in the Eucharist, when Jesus comes to us and is really present, body and blood, soul and divinity. Through this sacred ritual, Jesus lives among us and perpetually gives his people the graces necessary for salvation.

The eucharistic liturgy must be the focal point of community faith and the incentive for youth to recognize the role of faith in their lives. When this is absent, it is easier for young people to search for happiness in all the wrong places—material and secular things—and miss the real source of happiness, that is found at the heart of faith and in God's ongoing gift of the Eucharist, the heart of the Christian community and the place where we share the good news of God's love.

A New Awakening of Faith

Ministry of Service

The ministry of service is the third component of evangelization. Here, what is proclaimed through the word of God and celebrated in worship is carried out in service. Hence, ministerial actions complete the circle of evangelization.

From the beginning of Christianity, the Church has reached out to the poor and needy. Jesus proclaimed in the synagogue in Nazareth:

> The Spirit of the Lord is upon me,
>   because he has anointed me
>   to bring good news to the poor.
> He has sent me to proclaim release to the captives
>   and recovery of sight to the blind,
>   to let the oppressed go free. (Luke 4:18).

In other words, Jesus came to alleviate the suffering of humanity, whether that suffering be spiritual, physical, psychological, or material.

Through the centuries, good Christians have continued this commitment. This can be seen, for example, through the missionary work of St. Elizabeth of Hungary, St. Francis of Assisi, St. Teresa of Calcutta, Dorothy Day, and thousands of other men and women who have dedicated their lives to serving the poor in soup kitchens and various ways. Finally, we find Christ's call to serve the poor in the witness of millions of mothers and fathers who sacrifice their time and talent to serve their families and neighbors.

If we look for an entrance point to motivating our youth to appreciate the Catholic faith and recognize the value of Jesus's words today, a great place to begin is with the service ministries of the Church. Young adults have a strong attraction to service. They often volunteer their time and talent with nonprofit organizations to assist the needy in various parts of the world through various social endeavors. When I taught at the university level, I was impressed by the number of young adults who gave a year or more of their lives to go to needy parts of the world to assist in service projects.

Furthermore, young people respond well to those needing help. Connecting this call with their Catholic faith enhances their desire to find out more about the Church and become part of the Church's efforts to bring equality to all people in the world. The Church's social ministry is strong and can show those who come after us that the Church has much to offer them and society.

This same desire to serve can also be applied to the commitment of our younger generation to treat the earth with care and respect. Pope Francis urges us to treat the planet with dignity and to respect all creation. Once again, when our young people realize that this is an important aspect of the Church's mission and ministry, they respond favorably for it resonates with their needs and desires. Consequently, evangelization includes treating all of God's creation with respect and reverence.

FOR DISCUSSION

We now consider how passing on the faith involves a new evangelization.

A New Awakening of Faith

1. What small ways can evangelization happen in your home, the domestic church?

2. How do families fulfill their missionary mandate with their children and by reaching out to neighbors and associates?

3. Discuss how to address different opinions on sensitive moral matters with your spouse, children, friends, parents, or students.

4. What advice can you give parents who want to pass on their faith to their children?

5. What obstacles do changing approaches to the truth present for civil society and the Church?

6. What ways can you nurture the role and importance of prayer, including the rosary, in your home and community so that you build a strong foundation for family?

7. Discuss with your family or class what it means to treat all of God's creation with respect and reverence.

10

VIBRANT PARISHES, FAITHFUL FAMILIES

A vibrant parish begins with faithful families, as children assimilate the values inherent in their homes, the domestic churches. The Church depends on these domestic churches to be strong if it is to be fruitful and pass on the faith to future generations. Consequently, parishes need to assist families since the home is the first community of faith. This final chapter addresses ways that the parish and family can work together to overcome the challenges of materialism and secular society so that parish communities remain alive and well.

All communities are built on relationships. Some spring from belonging to certain ethnic groups or neighborhoods, others emerge from being members of a sports team. There are also professional communities that develop randomly, like attorneys, doctors, or teachers, who come together with like-minded professionals. Catholic parish communities are based on membership in the Catholic Church.

When I was a boy, our parish community was composed mostly of Irish and German families. When my ancestors settled in Cincinnati, they joined ethnic parishes—Germans in one parish, Irish in another. Many Catholics of other ethnicities did likewise. The spirit and dynamic of a parish were strongly influenced by its ethnic composition.

Gradually this changed, as English became the common language of immigrants to the United States and parishes integrated people from various ethnic groups. As this happened, parishes flourished and reached their zenith during the second half of the twentieth century.

In this current century, as the demographics have changed and people have moved to other parts of the country, the number of Catholics in many parishes has declined. Along with these changes, an ever-increasing material and secular culture, including social media, is increasingly making demands on people's energy and time.

Today, people must make an intentional decision to participate in the life of their parish. For this reason, pastors and church leaders need to be more attentive to the spiritual needs of their congregation, give stronger support to the domestic churches of the home, and develop small faith communities within the parish.

VIBRANT COMMUNITIES OF FAITH

Parishes are more than efficient organizations with definite goals, objectives, and nicely worded mission statements. While these assist active parish communities, faith formation includes more than developing new programs and establishing efficient parish organizational structures.

The Future of Catholicism

For parishes to attract and maintain new members, the following actions are important:

- *Responding to parishioners' needs.* Parishes exist to worship God and serve people in various ways. Multiple studies indicate that successful parishes know their parishioners' needs and respond to them.
- *Committing to family ministry.* The first home of Christian learning is located in the family. From the time couples are engaged and plan for their marriage, they need to include prayer, a Catholic environment, faith formation, and a commitment to parish liturgical activities as important parts of their future families.
- *Growing as a spiritual community.* A Catholic family is centered around Christ. An intentional decision to make him the focal point of family life is the best way to begin a domestic church. A family needs to know that God is with them through their joys and difficulties, providing a spiritual path for the family to follow.
- *Connecting liturgies with people's lives.* Pastors and liturgists have about an hour each week at Mass to inspire parishioners. The homily is a vibrant part of connecting liturgy with the personal and family needs of parishioners. This applies to Sunday Mass and other liturgies, where the presider, liturgist, and ministers address the congregation's needs through prayer and the mysteries celebrated. In so doing, parishioners better connect

Vibrant Parishes, Faithful Families

what happens at Mass with what is occurring in their lives.
- *Developing a sense of welcome.* When not presiding at Sunday Mass, I often go to Mass in neighboring parishes, where I am not known. After doing this for several years, I can say that I have never been greeted or welcomed by anyone in the churches that I have visited. It is no wonder that some visitors to a parish do not return! Welcoming a stranger can be an entry point for further involvement in the parish. In our impersonal world, people need to feel welcome. When it is absent, an opportunity is missed.
- *Providing spiritual activities for children and youth.* Time to attend Mass and parish catechetical and ministerial activities often competes with family time spent in sporting activities and other youth functions. To address this competition, parents often help children prioritize what is important. There are many opportunities for young people to engage in secular activities. Consequently, parishes must provide quality programs and spiritual activities for their young members. Parish leaders need to work with youth leaders to discern what spiritual activities motivate their young people to become involved in the parish, including the liturgy, choir, social ministries, or other activities such as food pantries, visiting the sick and elderly, and volunteering to assist the needy.
- *Offering vibrant catechesis.* Faith formation is generally more effective if it includes family

components, since the home environment is at the heart of young people's maturation in faith. While the parish needs to support the parents, the parents need to encourage their children to participate in what the parish offers by way of catechesis and service projects. Both complement each other and prepare children to be knowledgeable and faithful Catholics through teaching and good example.
- *Celebrating major feasts and seasons.* Epiphany and Pentecost provide occasions for parishioners to celebrate with potluck dinners and engage in other social gatherings. Celebrations during Advent and Lent may include fish fries. During such seasons, parishes can provide opportunities for families and young people to gather socially and remind parishioners of the feast that they celebrate.
- *Offering person-centered leadership.* Person-centered pastors lead vibrant parishes. As we have noted earlier, a parish is a faith community, not merely an efficient organizational structure. People need to feel welcome, and the pastor and the pastoral staff need to be available. Parish leaders may not have charismatic personalities, but a parishioner instinctively knows when they care. This happens through pastoral presence in the liturgy and personal encounters, like sickness and death. It is also evident in their availability for sacramental celebrations and other activities.

Vibrant Parishes, Faithful Families

A FAMILY FOCUS

Family ministry is the key to the success of future parishes. Today, it has become increasingly important to recognize the role that parents play in future parish vitality and in the faith formation of their children.

This role requires parents to make intentional decisions to create a family focus and a Catholic environment in their home. In the case of mixed marriages, this means that parents of different religious denominations decide what spiritual values are fundamental for their families and incorporate them into their home environment. In making these intentional decisions in the home, the parish can assist families by:

- Helping them grow as a domestic church and all it implies.
- Helping the parents grow together in their relationship with each other and in their faith.
- Helping parents identify and carry out their role as missionary disciples.
- Encouraging parents to pray together and with their families to create a Catholic home environment.
- Helping parents and families through catechesis learn to live the basics of their faith at home.
- Encouraging visible signs of their faith in their homes, including the Bible, a crucifix, the rosary, other religious symbols and prayers, and so on.
- Stressing the social mission of the Church in response to Christ's call to work with the poor and needy.

The Future of Catholicism

- Encouraging small groups of Catholics to come together to pray, study scripture, and discuss the fundamentals of the faith.
- Using social media to develop Internet discussion groups for children and teenagers on social ministry and other items of interest.

To create a vibrant Church is challenging. Through the combined efforts of Church members, however, it can happen. Let us pray that our parishes are filled with faithful Catholics.

FOR DISCUSSION

We now consider how vibrant parish communities, focusing on the family, are needed to pass on the faith.

1. In our rapidly developing world, why is it important to set aside time to attend Mass, reflect on the deeper realities of life, and communicate them to our loved ones?

2. Do you think that a person's faith is nurtured in the home and family? Why?

3. What are the many challenges and implications of social media for parish leaders today?

4. What are the challenges and implications of technology and social media for family life and passing on our faith?

5. What technological issues offer opportunities for growth for families and church communities?

6. What role do immigrants have for the future of Catholicism in the United States?

7. In what ways does your parish provide a family focus and in what ways can it improve this focus for the future revitalization of your parish community?

CONCLUSION

It is a joyful experience to see active, energetic parishes with people of all ages. It is also disheartening to know that there are Catholics who become disillusioned and leave the Church. The latter emotion results from my conviction that the Catholic Church offers all the spiritual means necessary to gain happiness here and salvation for eternity.

A positive attitude toward faith can be supported and enhanced by studying the history of the Church through the centuries. The same attitude is reflected in religious art, music, and architecture, which form statements of faith by the artists and those who commissioned their works. This same history includes documents defending the rights of the poor and workers, the existence of holy people, all of which have been motivated by the person, Jesus Christ.

As we reflect on the Church's accomplishments, we can be proud of the many saints and holy men and women who followed their call to proclaim the good news to all people, as well as the ordinary people—religious and lay—who continue to support the message of Jesus and the mission of the Church.

Of course, there are and always have been different approaches to proclaiming Jesus's message. These are reflected in the Gospels and the liturgical rituals of the Western and Eastern churches. They are also manifested in the charisms of the various religious orders, including the Franciscans,

Conclusion

Dominicans, Jesuits, and other religious communities. Even approaches to fundamental teachings such as the nature of grace and other theological issues have varied by Catholic theologians like Saints Augustine and Thomas Aquinas.

Through the centuries, popes and bishops have guided the Church, teaching faithfully what is rooted in the Scriptures and sacred Tradition. Religious men, women, and pastors have guided the faithful through changing times in the Church always mindful that it is the Holy Spirit who leads the Church and instills it with life and vitality. It is this dynamism of vitality that continues to be inherent in the call of the Holy Spirit to change the face of the Church through all its members. May God bless their ministry as they work to heal a broken world!

SELECTED BIBLIOGRAPHY

PRIMARY SOURCES

Aquinas, Thomas. *Summa Theologiae*. Translated by Fathers of English Dominican Province. London: Burns Oates and Washbourne, 1920.

Baltimore Catechism. New York: Colorado Springs, CO: Benziger Brothers, 1949, 1952.

Catechism of the Catholic Church. Washington, DC: USCCB, 1994 and 1997.

Code of Canon Law. Washington, DC: Canon Law Society of America, 1983.

Family Perspective in Church and Society. Washington, DC: USCCB, 1988 and 1998.

Francis, Pope. *Amoris laetitia* (On Love in the Family). Post-synodal Apostolic Exhortation. Vatican City, Libreria Editrice Vaticana, 2016.

———. *Evangelii Gaudium* (Joy of the Gospel). Encyclical. Vatican City: Libreria Editrice Vaticana, 2013.

Pope Paul VI. *Humanae vitae* (Of Human Life). Encyclical. Vatican City: Libreria Editrice Vaticana, 1968.

Second Vatican Council. *Lumen gentium* (Dogmatic Constitution on the Church). Collegeville, MN: Liturgical Press, 1975.

———. *Sacrosanctum Concilium* (Constitution on the Sacred Liturgy). Collegeville, MN: Liturgical Press, 1975.

Synod on Synodality. *Instrumentum laboris* (For a Synodal Church: Communion, Participation, Mission). Vatican City: Holy See Press Office, 2023.

SECONDARY SOURCES

Burns, James McGregor. *Leadership*. New York: Harper and Row, 1978.

Hater, Robert J. *Common Sense Catechesis: Lessons from the Past, Road Map for the Future*. Huntington, IN: Our Sunday Visitor Press, 2014.

———. *The Parish Guide to the New Evangelization: An Action Plan for Sharing the Faith*. Huntington, IN: Our Sunday Visitor Press, 2013.

———. *Your [Imperfect] Holy Family: See the Good, Make It Better*. Cincinnati, OH: Franciscan Media, 2015.

Kuhn, Thomas S. *The Structure of Scientific Revolutions*. Chicago: University of Chicago Press, 1962, 2012.

Milton Keynes UK
Ingram Content Group UK Ltd.
UKHW021027170924
448459UK00014B/597